CONTENTS

GW00758818

ISBN: 1 871947 23 5
PUBLISHED BY

12 MILLFIELDS CLOSE, KILGETTY
PEMBROKESHIRE SA68 0SA
TEL: (01834) 813991 FAX: (01834) 814484

FOREWORD

I n my years as Director of the Passenger Shipping Association I came to know Olau Line and its management team well. They were active members of the Association and totally supportive of any proposal that promoted the concept of ferry travel.

The fact that their General Manager, Case Rietkerk, served as both Chairman of the PSA Ferry section as well as Chairman of the Association meant that I had ample opportunity to observe both their operating standards and management style, both of which I highly approved.

It is therefore both a pleasure and a sorrow to supply these few words to this account of the 'life and death' of a first class ferry Company. Alan Ogilvie, the author, is uniquely qualified to write the Olau story having served the line during almost the entire period of its existence - virtually from start to wind up.

His story is told in a frank 'warts and all' manner that was typical of the Olau management style and although I do not agree with everything he writes, I commend the book as thoroughly entertaining and instructive.

The standards set by Olau Line both in terms of tonnage and service are those by which all Companies engaged in the Ferry Industry will be subsequently measured.

I am told the most common epitaph observed in graveyards is 'gone but not forgotten'. This most affectionate farewell could be justly applied to Olau Line.

Ken Page

September 1994

INTRODUCTION

Olau was not just another Ferry Company neither is this another ferry book. It is a living tribute to all the former managers, staff, and crew at Olau Line, who together helped us create the best ferry service in the country. Over 11 million passengers and nearly 1 million freight units, over the years, voted with their feet for something different from the many cross Channel cattle boats that were contemporary with the commencement of our service.

From day one I started taking pictures, ending up with several thousand when the Line finally closed on the 15th May 1994. Anyone can take photographs, but I tried to take pictures that told a story. At every Company land mark I tried to be there. Furthermore, I also inherited our Sales department photographic archive, which together with other pictures that have come my way over the years, forms the basis of this book. All the pictures in this book are from my own personal archive unless otherwise stated.

My first day at Olau Sheerness was the 13th July 1975 as an employee of Binder Hamlyn, the Chartered Accountants to Olau Line Akts, Denmark. It was a beautiful sunny day and my initial impression, as head of the audit team, was of a fledgling organisation struggling under the weight of an explosion of new business.

At Sheerness Docks a ferry terminal was under construction but not yet completed nor open, so there were no facilities for passengers - just a few portacabins and a building site. The weather however was uncharacteristically kind with wall to wall sunshine which continued most of the summer. This new Sheerness-Vlissingen ferry operation had started on the 20th November 1974 as a freight only service, managed by Bluett Shipping on behalf of Olau Line, Denmark.

Binder Hamlyn had been brought in to conduct an accounting investigation on behalf of Olau Line Denmark following Bluett's discovery of a massive fraud by one of their employees. On the face of things the fraud did not extend to Olau's operation but from the 1st July 1975 however, Ole Lauritzen, the proprietor, who was very much a hands-on owner, was moved to take over direct control of the whole operation through Olau Line (UK) Ltd.

The colossal growth was constantly outstripping all of the systems but one thing became rapidly clear - the enthusiasm of all associated with the operation was electric. Here was something new, something different, a living Company, a usurper, coming from nowhere and questioning the status quo. At the time Townsend Thoresen thought and probably were, the country's top ferry service embodying the spirit of a new age of continental motor travel. Ole knew he could do better and set about trying to do so.

Case Rietkerk joined the Company in September 1975, and rapidly became General Manager. We immediately got on and quickly formed an alliance determined to get things done, and make Olau Line the best ferry service in the country. After a number of approaches, I finally decided to take the plunge and accepted the appointment of Financial Controller, joining Olau Line officially in March 1976 although having been almost permanently seconded through Binder Hamlyn since July 1975.

Right from the start Ole Lauritzen wanted a different kind of service, a service where people came first, and at last had a choice. Although Ole was unable, through lack of resources, to develop his theme and the route to its full potential, it was his vision and his flagrant disregard for convention and so called experts that established the route in the first place.

The Line was acquired by a German consortium in 1978 to be untimely destroyed in March 1994 by an act of industrial vandalism by members of the German crew workers' participation council, who did for Olau Line what 'Red Robbo' did for British Leyland in the 1970's.

As Case Rietkerk succinctly put it 'The Unions have succeeded where our competitors have failed, put us out of business'.

Read and enjoy the Olau story. You will not see its like again.

Alan Ogilvie

October 1994

SHEERNESS
DAILY RO/RO SERVICE
FLUSHING

SAILING TIMES
Depart Sheerness 22.00 hrs. Arrive Flushing 07.00 hrs.
Depart Flushing 11.00 hrs. Arrive Sheerness 18.00 hrs.

- Sailing 7 days a week

- Capacity - 22 trailers + 35 cars
  (inc. 12 accompanied drivers)

 # OLAU-LINE

LIMITED - SHIP OWNERS
CHANNEL FERRY DIVISION

SHEERNESS AGENTS:
BLUETT SHIPPING LIMITED,
FERRY TERMINAL BUILDING,
SHEERNESS DOCKS,
SHEERNESS, KENT.
Telephone: Sheerness 61251
Telex: 965249

VLISSINGEN (FLUSHING) AGENTS:
N. V. HAVEN VAN VLISSINGEN
BINNENHAVEN,
VLISSINGEN (FLUSHING)
NETHERLANDS.
Telephone: (01184) 5096
Telex: 55241

Ring Bill Moses at Sheerness 61251 for full details

The first advertisement for the new Olau Ferry service as it appeared in International Freight Weekly on the 27th November 1974

Chapter 1

OLAU LINE

The actual structure of Olau Line was a mystery to many people, particularly those who obtained a copy of our accounts from Companies House.

Olau Line (UK) Limited was formed in July 1975 as the operating Company of the ferry service Sheerness to Vlissingen. It was effectively Line Agent managing all aspects of the line and remitting surplus funds to the holding company, at that time Olau Line Akts in Denmark. Olau Line Akts owned or chartered the ships that operated on the route. Ole Lauritzen owned the **Olau East, Olau West** and **Olau Kent** through his Danish Company whilst the **Olau Finn** was chartered from Oy Finnlines.

When we were acquired, in 1978, by the German consortium, the shares in Olau Line (UK) Limited were transferred to Trampschipfart Geselshaft of Hamburg and later to Kanalfahrdienst Olau Line also in Hamburg. From the time of the German acquisition, Olau Line (UK) Limited acted purely as line agent and instead of retaining income and expenditure in its own books, transferred all income and expenditure at the end of each year to the holding company in Hamburg. In return it received a fixed annual commission or agency fee of £15,000 of which half was liable to Corporation Tax. This extraordinary arrangement was agreed with the Inland Revenue on the basis that everything we did was on behalf of the head office so there was no real trade as such within the Company. All the assets and liabilities however of both Sheerness and Vlissingen were held in the UK books

to facilitate the ability of the Company to trade.

The German built ships **Olau Hollandia** 1 & 2, and the **Olau Britannia** 1 & 2, were actually individually owned by Partenreederei's, unlimited partnerships which is a special tax status in Germany. In fact the actual share holdings of each ship were slightly different although the major shareholders remained the same.

A Partenreederei is a special arrangement whereby a group of people or companies come together to guarantee the finance required to build a ship; they take a percentage of the total cost, say 20%, and put up the necessary collateral. The finance is raised, the ship is built and enters the trade for which it was designed. If the ship trades at a profit our fictitious shareholder would get 20% of it but his liability is unlimited for 20% of any loss incurred as well.

In practice, if this works right, the ship trades, the loan is repaid from positive cash flow and at the end of the day our shareholder owns 20% of the value of the ship which if maintained properly is usually more or less what it cost to build. This is significantly different to UK law where partnership liability is joint and several which means partners have unlimited liability for all debts of the partnership not just their agreed share.

The arrangement, which is unique to shipping in Germany, is not a lot unlike a Lloyd's syndicate whereby only guarantees are put up and income or profits (or losses) derive from this. Each

Olau Britannia (1) and **Olau Britannia** (2) side by side in Vlissingen on the 21st May 1990. The old Britannia has just completed her last voyage with Olau and will sail shortly to the Baltic for delivery to her new owners, Fred Olsen (now Color Line) to become the m.v **Bayard**.

Partenreederei had its own books and accounts and the income and expenditure from Olau Line (UK) Limited was allocated accordingly.

At Olau in Sheerness we ran the operation on a very small management team of just seven managers who were expected to have, apart from their specialist expertise, a broad working knowledge of the whole business. I always likened working at Olau to playing with a big train set but more fun.

The key of course was that we all enjoyed a very much hands-on job. THE ONLY PLACE FOR PASSENGERS WAS ON THE SHIPS. Nobody was allowed to stand on their dignity and all the staff knew we would not ask them to do something we were not prepared to do ourselves.

The hours were long and the job required a more than total commitment: if the phone rang in the night it always meant trouble. Although we were German owned the day to day running of the business rested with the managers in Sheerness and Vlissingen with Board control being exercised on capital expenditure, policy, budgets, tariffs and group computer development.

Each of us had a specialist brief and section to run but Case Rietkerk encouraged managers and staff to be free thinking. The result was an organisation that belonged to all of us, we had all developed it to where it was over the years. Most things were done for a known reason after taking input from all involved in a particular aspect of our business. Change could be achieved rapidly in brainstorming sessions if circumstances so dictated and in everything we did, attention to detail and customer service was the order of the day.

I have personally always felt that in a well run small Company, such as Olau, there is no place for a Union which I have always viewed as a protection club for the weak and a reflection on bad management to staff communication. At Olau in Sheerness we had a small Transport and General Workers Union representation and although we had a collective bargaining agreement with them we hardly saw them year in year out in the last eight years; although they were of course involved in the redundancy packages on the closure of the line.

The danger with unions, always, is that the membership can get hijacked by a few bigots who do not truly represent the membership at all or who superimpose their own selfish considerations which prevail. What management say to unions is sadly often misrepresented by either ignorant or selfish shop stewards as it is passed on to the members; it is always better that management speak to staff direct then there is no doubt as to what is said or meant.

At Olau, on the shore side the two shop stewards' jobs were actually press ganged positions; all the individual Union members wanted the job done but were not prepared to do it themselves, it was like being a hangman. This of course could be a mixed blessing as well at times.

When Olau closed we had built up a team of 103 people whose faces still haunt me as Case informed them of the start of our problems which would prove to be fatal.

They all looked at us in stunned disbelief when we informed them of the first signs of trouble coming from the Seebetriebsraat (on board German workers' participation council). Not one of them had a warning on file and the whole operation had been running like a Swiss Watch with a record year in prospect.

Of course as managers we knew of the troubles with the Seebetriebsrat and that a time bomb was ticking. We all knew that a showdown was inevitable sooner or later, with probably some blood letting, but complete closure shocked us as well.

All the staff are now gone and soon Olau will blend into history but in this book I have tried to show something of the special nature of how the business was created. It was part of all of us.

The completed new Olau Ferry Terminal at Sheerness in May 1988.

Chapter 2

SHORE OPERATIONS

SHEERNESS AS A FERRY PORT

Sheerness, as a Royal Dockyard at the junction of the Thames and Medway enjoyed a strategic position, although it never quite reached the eminence of Chatham which outlived it until 1983. The Royal Naval Dockyard of Sheerness finally closed in 1960 although many had seen the writing on the wall before then.

Following closure by the Admiralty, the port was run as several independent Companies which were brought together in October 1969 by the creation of the Medway Ports Authority, (MPA) a public utility or Trust Port.

In late 1974 Ole Lauritzen had been casting around for a new Port in the UK for a 'freight only' service to Vlissingen and settled on Sheerness mainly because everyone else had discounted it. In 1974 there were no facilities and many of the old Royal Dockyard buildings were hastily being demolished before preservationists got a look in. From a port owners' point of view, old buildings, particularly listed buildings, do not earn their keep, they take up space, are expensive to maintain and can rarely be put to economical use.

As a Public Authority, the MPA was starved of investment capital. It could not mortgage its assets to raise money as the assets, then at least, belonged to all of us, the tax payers. Their only option was to borrow forward against anticipated income, and although this was a perfectly normal way to raise finance, the actual funds that banks would make available using this method were considerably restricted.

Into this environment entered Ole Lauritzen, a man who knew what he wanted and whose Danish/English dictionary did not include the word 'no'. There were no usable assets apart from a link span and pontoon bridge, and no infrastructure just earth and footings of hastily demolished buildings. Ole needed a terminal and hard standing in a hurry as the ferry was booming, but as the Port had no funds nor adequate means to

An aerial view of Sheerness Docks looking towards the Isle of Grain in March 1993. **Olau Hollandia** (2) is on her new berth and most of the other berths in the Port have ships in. The Port of Sheerness has made itself a major importer of cars but also handles fruit, timber, paper and steel in large quantities. The old Royal Dockyard is the area to the right of the picture. In the centre foreground is Sheerness Steel which occupies the old Dockyard sports ground whilst the large car standing area to the left, the Lappell Bank, has been reclaimed from the estuary. (Olau collection)

The Port of Sheerness is situated on the North West coast of the Isle of Sheppey which is connected to mainland Kent by the Kingsferry Bridge. This bridge is the only link to the mainland and carries a single carriageway road and one railway line. It lifts on average eight times a day for shipping and in this view looking West the m.v. **Cambeck**, a dredger bound for Ridham Dock, is passing through in March 1993. (Olau collection)

on the part of the Port, since most of what Olau provided could not be realistically removed; they knew that if they did nothing, we would have to, which we duly did until the end.

Sheerness Docks in the 1970's was much different from that of today. The stevedores were not employed by the Port but by the National Dock Labour Scheme, which gave them a so called job for life and virtually made them discipline proof. All the other scheme ports were having tremendous labour problems at this time. The Port of London was in terminal decline whilst Dover and Felixstowe, non scheme ports, were prospering although they too had their occasional problems with strikes.

Sheerness however bucked the trend, here was a scheme port with a good industrial relations record but this was achieved at a price. The price was expensive labour and inefficient work practices but it was not all bad news. Sheerness had rapidly gained a reputation for reliability against a background of uncertainty elsewhere and as a consequence it prospered.

By late 1986 it was becoming apparent that our Ferry

raise funds at that time, he paid for them himself and thereby started a tradition that continued until our closure in May 1994.

The name Olau incidentally was derived from Ole's name thus - O. LAUritzen. The most common corruptions of which were Olav Line, and Oola Line (popular with dyslexic travel agents).

Olau opened the new terminal on 8th November 1975, provided a small baggage hall, and concreted the coach park. Within a year we had built our own walkway and gangway to the ship, all on the back of the Port pleading poverty or parsimony. Initially all passenger transfers from the terminal to the ship were by transfer bus which was inefficient, expensive and time wasting, but necessary, for safety as it being a bonded area.

In fact this policy was very shrewd in the short term

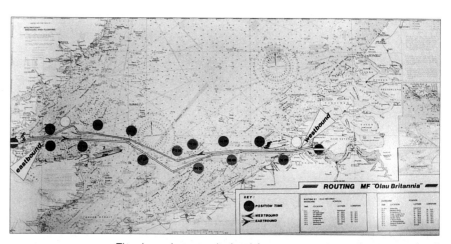

The above chart was displayed for many years in our ferry terminal and showed the ships' routes to Vlissingen and times en route. Both Sheerness and Vlissingen are on the same line of latitude of 51 degrees 27 minutes North but the actual route was far from straight. The first deviation on leaving Sheerness was in the Thames Estuary through the North Edinburgh Channel which was necessary for two out of three sailings due to low water in the Princess Channel, the more direct route. The second detour was to cross the Channel separation lanes at 90 degrees. The English Channel is set up like an invisible motorway with East-West traffic using the English side and West-East traffic the French side. There is also a 'no mans' central reservation down the centre. Once through the separation lanes our route followed the Belgian coast to the Schelde Estuary and Vlissingen.

Terminal Building would require substantial renovation or reconstruction. The original building was of light construction and with its flat roof, purgatory to work in during the summer and like an ice box in winter. Costings established that there was not a lot of difference between the cost of repairs and a complete rebuild so a rebuild it was.

The new building was designed and built by Swale Construction and opened on time at Easter 1988. Olau's administration staff had moved from the old building six months earlier, in September 1987 to The Old Paymaster's House, one of the few surviving buildings from Royal Dockyard days. This building had been

The Medport News issue of November 1975 announcing the opening of the first Sheerness ferry terminal.

gutted by fire and was refurbished by Olau to its former glory.

The National Dock Labour scheme was finally abolished in May 1989 and the port privatised shortly afterwards by way of a Management Buy-out (MEBO). The new owners then quickly seized the opportunity to rationalise their labour force and sweep aside all of the restrictive practices and labour abuses of the earlier years. This was done in a very unusual manner resulting in many unsavoury incidents and virtually the whole workforce taking paid leave, (so called garden leave) before refusing to accept new contracts and resigning en masse; although arguably this was constructive dismissal.

Having rationalised its labour force with contract labour, the port owners maintained the pre scheme status quo by not passing any of the savings back to Olau who were finding it increasingly difficult to attract new business. Unbeknown to Olau at the time, the Port owners had their eye on their short term share price rather than on their long term customers.

In the meantime all the other ports in the UK were getting their act together; other ports knew the value of a customer, not only obtaining trade but keeping it. Everyone that is except the Port of Sheerness who stubbornly refused to pass cost savings back to Olau.

This constant refusal to be realistic caused Olau at the beginning of 1993 to start looking at its future viability and in particular another port option. At that time the dualling of the A249 from the M2 to the Kingsferry Bridge had not started neither had the long awaited improved docks entrance. A start on the dualling had been pledged in 1993 but this was slipping away, and with a huge budget deficit, and swingeing cuts to the roads programme in prospect, the future looked bleak if Olau chose to remain at Sheerness.

By mid 1993 Olau felt more trapped, being unable to materially reduce operating costs, and saddled with poor infrastructure whilst money was being spent everywhere else on roads with much less traffic, the A299 for example. Roads building in this country is nothing to do with need, it is manipulation and political clout that wins the day.

Olau's only options against this background was to trade our way out or move from Sheerness, but more of that later.

IMMIGRATION

Immigration Officers are provided free at all ports and Airports by the Home Office in London, and in addition they are often linked with Special Branch Officers who also oversee passenger movements on the look out for criminals and/or terrorists on the move.

In 1975, before the days of the EC, Immigration control for every non-British Passport holder was very strict and in particular visitors often had to show visible means of support ie cash before being allowed entry. It was effectively a mini Spanish Inquisition without Torquemada. The thinking behind this was that if an immigrant had no money, and no address to go to he/she was either going to work illegally, sponge off the State, or live on their wits, all of which were

Inside the new Sheerness ferry terminal. The design was airy and spacious, designed for minimum maintenance both inside and out.

socially undesirable. In particular every non-British foot passenger entering the country had an 'interview' with an Immigration Officer whilst car passengers were generally checked whilst sitting in their vehicles.

Passports had to be valid (ie not forgeries and not out of date), contain the correct visas if appropriate, and not contain any unauthorised amendments/alterations or indeed UK deportation stamps. Trained Immigration Officers can scrutinise passports in seconds but any irregularities cost the

Case Rietkerk pointing out to me that photography is not permitted in the Immigration Hall

carrier, dearly. There is no charge for Immigration services any hour of the day or night but any person that is refused must be detained pending deportation at the carrier's cost, in this case Olau. This could be extremely expensive, although most of the costs were recoverable under our P&I (Protection & Indemnity) Club insurance.

In 1977 a Filipino member of the **Olau Kent** crew somehow got into a fight in Sheerness with a Jamaican from a banana boat, resulting in the Jamaican ending up in hospital with a knife wound, and the Filipino in jail. It made sense for all concerned not to charge the Filipino but deport him instead. If charged and convicted he would have been detained at the cost of the UK tax payer and then be deported on release as he had no UK visa. He was visited in jail and invited to sign a paper allowing us to deduct his air fare from his crew wages. Although he understood the question his reply was something equivalent to 'go forth and multiply'. We took that as a 'yes' and the station sergeant signed the form on his behalf as the 'prisoner could not speak English'.

There were many ingenious attempts to smuggle people into the country over the years, most of which the authorities were wise to and usually ended in more deportations at our cost. One trick was for a small group, of ethnic extraction, to come ashore and clear

Immigration with correct visas and proper paperwork. One member of the party would then try and get back on board again saying he had lost something or someone and take back the paperwork used for the first group to be recycled. This invariably ended up in a mass deportation again at our cost.

For a while in the late 70's an underground student magazine 'recommended' a student dodge for Americans and Australians bumming round Europe. Immigration generally let these people into the UK if they had some money and an air ticket home. The racket was to enter the UK via a ferry, cash in the return half of your air ticket, and when your holiday was over purchase a return ticket on Olau to Vlissingen. The next step was to dope up on a prohibited substance before going through Customs or Immigration on returning to the UK, get stopped, and subsequently get deported home at the carrier's cost.

Another wangle, which is still rife, is for groups of people to arrive in the UK with proper visas either as part of a tour, usually the 'last' leg, or on 'holiday' or 'shopping'. Providing the group had correct paperwork and return air tickets they would be admitted but it was becoming increasingly apparent when most of them did not catch their return flights, that this was just another racket as well. In fairness technically some could have caught a later flight but nobody really believed that.

Olau had one tour operator who did this trick regularly with Malaysians and even schooled them on what to say to Immigration. The courier on the bus to London would ask if they were 'staying' thus releasing the air ticket returns for resale. At the time Immigration were powerless to stop this but following the two plane loads of Jamaicans who came into Gatwick for 'Christmas' shopping in 1993 things may now change.

Where a deportation notice was served on Olau we were obliged to repatriate the 'refusal' to the nearest country that would take them which was not necessarily

The approach to Immigration in Sheerness showing the segregation of EC and non EC passengers. The poles held rails which could be arranged to create queuing lanes and were known as the corral. On heavy sailings, to avoid crowds around the Immigration booths, passengers would queue through this arrangement. All passengers had to be presented to Immigration which involved our staffing the exit to the corral to release passengers one at a time.

Holland. A Dutchman, even if he was a mass murderer, would be deported to Holland as they had to take him being one of their own but other Nationals usually involved us in an escort to Heathrow and air tickets. Generally speaking the Immigration Authorities, both Dutch and English, were not that bothered who left their respective countries but once someone was refused on the other side, they would generally be refused at the port of departure as well.

Unless we wanted to keep these people on the ship ad infinitum our only option was to fly them back to their own country, or the nearest country that would take them, at our cost (no super APEX tickets here) plus of course pay for security accommodation and food before the flight. As mentioned earlier this was sometimes recoverable on our P&I Club insurance but not always, as we had a weekly and a monthly deductible figure which would depend on aggregation calculations.

In 1987 Margaret Thatchers's Government introduced an odious piece of legislation known as the 'Carriers Liability Act' and to add insult to injury John Major's Government in 1993 exempted the Channel Tunnel from its terms. Briefly under the terms of this Act every passenger who was presented to UK Immigration for entry to the UK without the proper paperwork incurred a fine of £1000 for the carrier. The ferries and Airlines, as industries, strongly fought this and were rewarded by it being doubled to £2000 in 1989. At the time no other EC country operated such a system. Since Olau only came from Holland these people were already in the EC. That was totally irrelevant as we were the 'offending carrier'; in truth it was a blatant tax nothing more nothing less.

Our only way out was to examine passenger documents on departure from Vlissingen but under Dutch Law we were not able to insist on examining passengers' personal travel documentation. We tried to circumvent this by having one of our staff in Sheerness additionally check travel papers of passengers before 'presentation' to an Immigration Officer in the UK and although this was useful it was not 100% effective.

Our fines were running at about £20,000 per annum in the end, but compared to other ferry operators and the airlines this was peanuts. The ferry operators through the Passenger Shipping Association (PSA) felt this was a case for a judicial review, as it was against the Treaty of Rome allowing free movement within the EC and unfair as other countries in the EC had no such Act.

However this was not to be as the last I heard was that similar Acts were being introduced in other EC countries: so much for the Treaty of Rome!

HM CUSTOMS & EXCISE

The role of HM Customs & Excise has dramatically changed over the last 20 years, thankfully mostly for the better.

Briefly the role of Customs is to protect the home country's trade, ensure all duty is paid where appropriate and by whatever means at their disposal enforce all fiscal and contraband regulations from bootleg booze to hard drugs and firearms trafficking.

The basic Customs Service is FREE which is the good news, but the bad news is that they only work Civil Service hours, ie from 8.30 a.m. to 4.30 p.m. five days a week. This was not a lot of use to a ferry operation. Work outside these hours is called '*special attendance*' and for this Olau had to pay. This was not cheap either as Olau had a ship in at 7.00 a.m. and a departure at 9.30 p.m. Special attendance was therefore a prerequisite unless we wanted to delay unloading until they turned up for work or alternatively

January 1985 and no Red and Green lane, just a White lane ! Nearly two feet of snow had fallen overnight and although the **Olau Hollandia** (1) could berth it was some three hours before it could unload. Customs, showing rare flexibility for the time, cleared vehicles in the newly created white lane.

we could sail empty.

We were in fact paying for the dubious privilege of slowing down our operation but without 'special attendance', port clearances would only take place during Civil Service normal hours. Game, set and match!

There were two main branches of Customs working from Sheerness, the ordinary officers and the so called black gang or rummage crew. The ordinary officers did the main paperwork and generally ran the Green and Red lanes at the Port, whilst the black gang ran their own show and went where they liked when they liked treading on whom they liked.

Above these two outfits were the revenue cutters who acted and behaved like roving pirates. They, like all Customs Officers, had enormous powers and on the few occasions we were visited they were extremely high handed and obnoxious. We never saw them again after John Major introduced his Citizens' Charter. For Customs & Excise, next to the Gas Board nobody needed it more than these guys.

In 1974 there was no Green or Red lane system just a single lane as at most other ports. Passengers arriving in Sheerness were all subjected to a mini Spanish Inquisition on entry. The Surveyor (the local senior customs officer) once proudly remarked to Case Rietkerk that they recovered more drugs in Sheerness than in any other port in the Country; Case politely pointed out this was a logical consequence as virtually everyone was at that time checked and it took ages to clear our ships.

In the late 70's the Red and Green channel arrangements at last came to Sheerness but for many years Customs still stopped every car for a personal interview. Case used to go through the Red lane in the end because it was quicker. Things gradually improved in the mid 80's and although all cars were still directed through the Customs shed many were waved straight out the other side.

During 1984 and 1985 we had been fighting a rearguard action with Customs as to our baggage reclaim area which they claimed was too small. This was brought to a head by their threatening to withdraw our port licence unless we did something about it so a new baggage hall it was.

Briefly foot passengers had an option to put their luggage on trolleys at both ports but this had to be reclaimed on arrival to go through Customs. Worse still however, Customs also required all coaches to be unloaded on arrival, all luggage reclaimed, walked with its owners through Customs, and back on the bus again.

This circus, fortunately, was not necessary in Holland, probably because there was nothing you could take in to the Netherlands that was not readily available there anyway.

In 1988, with the opening of the Common Market proper, Customs approached us and asked for official access to our booking computers. They already had this via our staff, but wanted a complete kit in their own

Mrs. Marguerite Rietkerk officially opens the new baggage reclaim hall on the 24th March 1986. Also in the picture left to right, Case Rietkerk (General Manager, Sheerness), Dieter Hartmann (General Manager, Vlissingen) The Mayor of Swale, the late Councillor Richard Morton and his wife Rose and Martin Bellmann. (Chief Executive Olau Line).

offices where they could work discreetly. Olau, in common with other ferry companies, had always co-operated fully with the various Government agencies, although on this occasion we only conditionally agreed to this request providing the access did not prove intrusive to our business. We had already allowed their TV cameras to be set up in our terminal with the proviso that we had access to their video tapes if required.

In fact the surprising consequence of this computer access was the opposite to what we expected. By accessing our sailing lists in good time, Customs knew exactly who they wanted to talk to before the ship docked, and at last after all these years the Green channel finally came into its own and most passenger cars bypassed the Customs shed completely.

Customs like most Government departments are very union oriented and on the few rare occasions they went on strike, it had a dramatic effect on the clearance time of the ships. It was on these occasions very slick indeed. On one occasion passengers were invited to estimate any duty payable and drop the money in an honesty box provided for the purpose. We never did find out how much was collected as to everyone's amusement someone pinched the box.

For operational purposes, Customs, from Olau's point of view, was split into three groups (excluding the VAT people) and each seemed to run their own little or in some cases big shows. What was immediately apparent was the obvious lack of communication between each, and the antipathy from those below to those above and just the arrogance of those above.

We had to try and work somehow with this lot but work it did. I once quizzed the local Surveyor in more or less the above terms as to why there was this apparent distrust even within their own people?

He likened the situation to unravelling a big ball of string with many ends: you do not know where something you start will end up, maybe another department is even holding the other end, but start you must and persevere you must. In those terms it sort of makes sense, but there must be an incredible amount of duplicated effort around. I wonder if they have ever heard of a computer data base?

The black gangs (oddly named as they wore dark blue) would arrive usually en masse complete with screw drivers, drugs dogs, boiler suits etc and target specific areas of our operations at random. On board these often involved taking parts of the ship to pieces and then not putting them back together, whilst ashore they would strip down motor vehicles or turn a whole load from a lorry. They went where they wanted and did what they wanted. They did however do a very good job and in more recent years the drugs busts particularly were well worth the effort, clearly based on excellent intelligence and with comparatively little inconvenience to other passengers.

The crew from the Revenue Cutter however were a different kettle of fish. Customs have a number of such cutters, I believe about eight, which patrol our coasts much on the lines of the American Coast Guard. These people seemed to have an unlimited brief and succeeded in souring our local Customs working relationship for weeks after they had been.

We were once fined £2000 by them for having a gaming machine switched on whilst in port. All un-licensed gaming machines had to be locked or electrically isolated whilst in port, but we were allowed to empty and service them. One such machine had just been repaired but was left switched on and momentarily unattended during a Customs Cutter visit. No passengers were on board but the machine played which technically broke the law, justifying their visit, hence the fine. The VAT people work on the same basis, they have to find something, albeit pennies, to show they have been and of course put us in our place. The Captain and I appealed against this as being totally unreasonable. The reply I received from the Cutter Officer in charge, which has unfortunately been destroyed now, or it would have been included in these pages, said something like 'how dare you question my right to do what I like'. Nice people.

January 1993 saw the biggest shake-up in our shore operation following the relaxation of virtually all Customs controls. We only came from another EC member state, Holland, and under the Common Market rules there were no tariff boundaries within the community. Cargo from outside the Community should have been cleared on entry into the EC but occasionally it arrived sealed and someone in the UK had to guarantee the duty. Our borders were now in places like Greece, and having been there this is most comforting to know!

Another unexpected bonus for us was that Duty Free allowances which had earlier been extended to 1999 were doubled under the new vendor control regulations which made Olau responsible for ensuring passengers only purchased their entitlement.

Suddenly, from 1st January 1993, we had traffic jams of cars and lorries leaving the docks whereas, previously the Customs slow release system had spread this out. The rules of the game were also changing with less emphasis on an individual customs officer's gut feeling but a more scientific approach using modern technology. Our baggage reclaim however, built at a cost of £1.7 million at Customs insistence, now became a white elephant, as being purpose-built and strategically placed it was totally useless as anything else.

In the end though we must not forget, England is an Island and as such the only member of the European Community that can control its borders. Rule Britannia!

PILOTAGE

The Thames Estuary from North East Spit (off Margate) to Sheerness is an area of compulsory pilotage as is the approach to Vlissingen up the River Schelde estuary from about 30 miles out. As a consequence, from its inception Olau Line was obliged to take pilots on both sides every day at an enormous cost to the Company.

From Sheerness we needed a Medway Pilot to the Medway Buoy then a Thames (or mud) pilot to North East Spit, although in practice one pilot covered both duties. Initially we landed the pilots by way of a launch off Margate, but slowing a ship to do this is time consuming and expensive on a daily basis. We also had to pay for the launch in all weathers, day and night, and this was sometimes a dangerous exercise.

After some discussions we rearranged things to carry the pilot over to Holland so that he did both the outward and return pilotage as one job but over two consecutive days. Olau in return would provide meals, a cabin, and pay expenses. Although this was an improvement, in that it saved the launch fees, the cost of providing what amounted to one person per ship, which we neither wanted nor needed, was in the order of £120,000 per ship per annum in 1977. A lot of money today and a hell of a lot of money in 1977.

An effective closed shop for want of a better expression, was operated at the time by Trinity House, who prevented our Masters (Danish at the time) from obtaining pilotage certificates, although British

HRH Prince Philip, the Duke of Edinburgh and Master of Trinity House at Sheerness to open the new pilot station. I got into trouble with Special Branch for getting this close without security clearance.

Masters could apply for examination and exemption. Meanwhile Olau continued to be bled white with these exorbitant charges.

In reality the Pilotage Service and their charges were geared to provide a pool of Pilots on stand by to bring in any ship which may come over the horizon at any time day or night. We argued that Olau, as a ferry, was effectively a bus service operating to a timetable thereby removing the costly standby element, but the elder brethren of Trinity House would hear none of it.

The General Council of British Shipping had no problem with the status quo as their member Companies Captains could obtain exemption and this discrimination effectively made them more competitive. Storm clouds were brewing though and through the Passenger Shipping Association (PSA), at the instigation of Brittany Ferries the foreign owned ferries joined forces.

Brittany Ferries brought the matter to a head by withholding pilotage payments of some £250,000 from Trinity House who started legal action to recover it. This however quickly politically stalled as the French, who had hitherto allowed British Masters on Brittany Ferries ships in and out of French waters, threatened to withdraw this concession.

The French with their curious mixture of Nationalism and anarchy always seem to find ways of getting things done in a way that would just not happen anywhere else.

We at Olau tried to run the same argument but with the same situation in Holland as England, Trinity House was not under pressure and continued to protect their patch. A number of other ferry operators did however strike deals and paid a percentage of the pilotage dues in exchange for exemption. Progress for Olau however stalled again.

The 1980's dawned with no concessions from Trinity House who, like the print unions, and most other bastions of restrictive practices, were oblivious of the changing world around them and seemed resolved to fight to the death. The mood however in the PSA which represented all ferry and cruise operators was also hardening.

A delegation from the PSA lobbied the Transport Minister who refused to intervene with that time honoured government political phrase 'I hear what you say but.....' which is political jargon for 'go away you tiresome people'.

With closer ties with Europe looming the time was now ripe for change and through the enormous resources of the PSA membership, DFDS and Olau Line took the Transport Minister to Court for a judicial review in 1983 with two test cases of restrictive practices.

Mr Justice Nolan in his judgement found that both Trinity House and the Secretary of State for Transport had acted unlawfully in refusing to allow EC masters to sit UK pilotage examinations which was contrary to Article 86 of the Treaty of Rome. Furthermore he found that Trinity House were not empowered to do deals such as had been struck with some ferry operators in exchange for pilotage exemption.

The result of this judgement was to allow all EC masters to sit UK pilotage examinations with a consequential huge saving to Olau Line and a huge bill from the High Court. English Justice is usually fair in the end but never, ever cheap.

Following this judgement the Dutch authorities also capitulated and thus a very large debit was removed from Olau's profit and loss account. Most of the Pilots took this quite philosophically but a number of embittered hard liners seemed to have a motto of 'don't get mad get even' and used every opportunity to delay our service or show lack of flexibility every time the opportunity presented itself.

Happily these Pilots could be counted on one hand and were by far outnumbered by the many professional Pilots who showed every courtesy, which was reciprocated. Everyone had a job to do after all.

In recent years the responsibility for pilotage control has passed from Trinity House to approved local

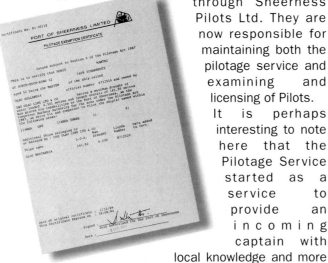

Captain Horst Mantei's last Pilotage Exemption Certificate issued by the Port of Sheerness covering both **Olau Hollandia (2) and Olau Britannia (2).**

harbour bodies which in the case of Sheerness is the Port of Sheerness Ltd., through Sheerness Pilots Ltd. They are now responsible for maintaining both the pilotage service and examining and licensing of Pilots.

It is perhaps interesting to note here that the Pilotage Service started as a service to provide an incoming captain with local knowledge and more particularly find his ship a berth in ports that were in those days very congested indeed. As ports got more organised and ships larger, navigation assumed greater importance and the service evolved to what it is today.

Any modern ferry service must operate with its officers holding pilotage exemption certificates as the daily cost at today's rates would make any business unviable. The Pilotage service as it has now evolved though still carries out a vital and professional function around our busy shores.

As a footnote there is reputed to be enormous sums of money sitting around the country in the various pilotage pots that technically should be redistributed back to those that paid it in. The custodians know it is not theirs, but are lost as to how should they go about redistributing it. Finding out just how much is salted away and who is custodian is probably going to be more difficult than trying to find the rest of the Brinks Mat bullion. Either way some of that money no doubt belongs to Olau.

LIGHT DUES.

Apart from the provision of Pilots, Trinity House were also responsible for many years for the collection of Light Dues. The whole of the UK is surrounded by lighthouses, buoys and a diminishing number of lightships. The upkeep of these came under Trinity House although the actual work was mainly carried out by the local harbours on their behalf. Collection of the Light Dues was by our old friends in Customs who usually insisted on seeing all the Ships' Papers which they were supposed to check. This put a stupid unreasonable burden on them as the Ships' Papers (all the Classification Society certificates) are usually in the home language of the Classification Society, in our case German. Even a dictionary is not always helpful as not only proper nouns have capital letters in German and they also have an annoying habit of joining words together in conjugation to make a more comprehensive incomprehensible word.

The payment method was a cunning ploy to generate maximum income. It was calculated on 'journeys' ie one trip in and one out, starting on 1st April with a maximum of three journeys a month and a maximum of

The **Nore Lightship** was positioned at the junction of the Thames and Medway just off Sheerness. As a claim to fame the Nore apart from hosting an infamous mutiny was also the site of the world's first lightship placed there in 1732. This, the last **Nore Lightship**, was positioned just North of No 1 buoy in the Medway Estuary, before being retired in the early 60's to be preserved in St. Katharine's Dock, London.

13 'journeys' a year. This gave exemption for the whole year to 31st March. You could pay the whole lot up front of course or on a monthly basis until exempt for the year. If we changed ships in say October we would be caught for a whole year on both ships. The **Olau Hollandia** (2) light dues, calculated on net tonnage and classification were around £80,000 per year which comprises the maximum of 13 journeys. One visit per year of say a cruise ship of the same tonnage would cost therefore one thirteenth or £6,153, whilst the daily rate over a whole year comes down to as little as £219 per day.

Trinity House whilst retaining the responsibility for lights are in the process of finding alternate methods of collection such as local harbours so that in future everyone down to small yachts will pay something. I wonder if someone has remembered they should be multi-linguists, as well, if they are to continue to examine Ships' Papers?

PORT HEALTH

One of the unsung heroes of the Port before the days of the European Community was the Port Health facility. However since 1st January 1993 and the opening of borders within the EC their role has considerably diminished.

The Port Health Service in Sheerness was free and came under the jurisdiction of the Corporation of the City of London. They had a general watching brief to ensure all food that entered the country was fit for human consumption and a wider brief that included the ship's operation itself and hygiene in the docks and onboard ship.

Briefly all meat for human consumption when being transported must be accompanied by certificates giving details of the number of the slaughter house, where it was prepared together with a health certificate confirming it is fit for human consumption.

For many years this information was also stamped on the meat but a tariff racket grew up around importing, exporting and re-importing meat to get Common Market subsidies more than once. This was achieved by over-stamping the original stamps of origin. Port Health got wise to this and started using different inks so the racketeers cut off the old stamp and replaced it with a new one.

The first check therefore was to see that the meat had not been round once before; it was then counted and the number of carcasses or boxes checked to the accompanying paperwork. The Certificate of health and origin is known as a Phytosanitary Certificate (PHYTO). Plants as well as foodstuffs entering the UK required a PHYTO Certificate.

All imported meat was checked and generally chilled meat was quickly cleared. Frozen meat, particularly prawns and shellfish however, was always tested and a block would be selected at random for defrosting and chemical analysis. The lorry though would usually be allowed to proceed to its destination subject to the cargo not being offered for sale until cleared. Problems were rare and usually the result of faulty refrigeration en route.

From the 1st January 1993 all foodstuffs imported from the EC could clear immediately providing it had a PHYTO Certificate and even foodstuffs from outside the EC could clear if a PHYTO Certificate was obtained on entering the EC or issued within the EC before entering the UK. These new regulations virtually eliminated this aspect of Port Health's responsibilities overnight unless there was a health scare on any particular item of food.

Port Health also had responsibilities on board ship

The Captain's buffet on **Olau Britannia** (1). With vast stocks of food required to produce this spread twice a day on board hygiene was essential. Port Health were responsible for regularly inspecting all food storage facilities on board ship.

for public health which remain unchanged. This is a care and attention brief which involved regularly checking all aspects of onboard cleanliness, checking for vermin, testing drinking water and the water in the swimming pool. Part of these requirements include the issue of a de-ratting certificate every six months for each ship certifying it to be vermin free.

All ships, or planes for that matter, are required, on arrival in the UK, to report any serious illness or death amongst passengers or crew to Port Health immediately. Port Health then have the right to quarantine the ship or plane for further investigation if the circumstances so justify. Problems were rare and even where a death had occurred on board the whole process was very slick and discreet.

England as everyone knows is an Island and as such has managed to avoid importing rabies which is prevalent across the whole of Europe but it is interesting that in Europe they do not regard rabies as a problem at all. Ironically our controls are now working in reverse as we now have mad cow disease in the UK and the Europeans are quite keen on us keeping it here.

The importation of any soft pawed animal into the UK is strictly forbidden unless it is first subjected to six months quarantine. At Olau we took a corporate decision not to officially import soft pawed animals under any circumstances, even for quarantine, although a few people were caught trying to smuggle animals over the years. There were no such restrictions on leaving the UK although Olau required passengers with animals to take a cabin and have a suitable container.

Dogs were strictly prohibited from the docks estate although Customs maintained kennels adjacent to our ferry terminal with special drugs sniffer dogs; these hounds always seemed permanently out of their brains on something when I saw them at work, perhaps it takes one to catch one?

Over the years Port Health tended to be the low key unsung heroes but one incident is immortalised for ever. In the summer of 1981 a duck, rather foolishly, decided to nest in the docks. Everyone was quite happy with this arrangement as it was something different. Everyone except Port Health that is who were none too pleased, as the nest with scraps of food would, they alleged, attract rats. The head of Port Health gave the instruction that the duck be apprehended and destroyed, a sentence which was duly carried out to the mortification of the stevedores who had by then adopted it.

The Sheerness stevedores always had subtle ways of making a statement so at Christmas they purchased a duck, cooked it, and solemnly marched into the office of the head of Port Health with it on a silver platter, placing it respectfully on his desk before retiring. Honour was satisfied although I doubt either duck saw the joke.

INSURANCE

Apart from the normal commercial insurances, Olau ships required two specialist insurances that were peculiar to shipping. These were ships 'hull insurance' and membership of a 'P&I Club'.

A ship, any ship, has to be self sufficient at sea which means it must have its own power supply, fresh

On almost the last day the **Olau Finn** was in service, Captain Seiko misjudged the tide and hit the Sheerness ramp making a hole some 4ft by 3ft in his stern. This was temporarily repaired by welding a plate inside the ship and filling the hole with quick setting cement with the ship actually sailing on time. The ship went off charter from Olau a few days later to be replaced by **Olau Britannia** (I). The hull underwriters would take care of the damage to the ship whilst the P&I Club would handle any third party claim from the Port.

'It fell off the back of a lorry guv'. Under the terms of our P&I Club insurance the Club carried the risk of the first journey from the ship and the last journey to the ship for trailers plus of course the voyage itself. Invariable in mishaps, it seemed that the cargo was always sticky or smelly (or both) as in the case with drums of, as I recall, impact adhesive. Not this kind of impact though!

This is done by the owners approaching a Classification Society, in Olau's case Germanica Lloyd, who survey every aspect of the ship, from its design, construction, and operation to safety equipment. The results of these surveys grant the ship a classification, (the highest London version is Al at Lloyds). Armed with a classification the owners can approach hull underwriters who will then accept the risk for an agreed premium. In practice the risk would be spread across many insurance syndicates but the risk would always be led off by a lead name who is an acknowledged expert in the particular risk (ferries, tankers, bulk carriers etc).

Hull underwriters surveyors are extremely strict and a surveyor can, if need be, order work to be done before a ship is permitted to put to sea. In practice this is in both the owners' and hull underwriters' interests to keep the ship in tip top condition at all times, A ship out of service is not earning money.

water, ventilation, sewage disposal system, and above all be safe. After all it is a small town in its own right. As a consequence modern ships are extremely expensive to build and operate, Olau's last ferries cost for example £55 million to build and around £45,000 a day each to run. This represents an enormous capital outlay and risk for the owners who obviously wish to insure their investment.

Olau's policy with its own built ships, was to always keep them in top condition which also maintained the resale value. The hull underwriters carry the risk of the ship itself including all machinery on board, it is just like house insurance in a way.

The actual risks carried by the P&I Club are the third

Apart from the special marine insurances Olau also carried enormous public liability policies for people and cargo in its care. In 1982 we obtained a major contract from General Motors for the importation of their cars made abroad. The Port of course screwed us on handling charges as at that time they had a restrictive practice that obliged the use of two sets of stevedores. An arrangement that was typical of the times. The cars were stored at our risk on pre-designated hard standing, or should have been. In practice they were put all over the place due to the double movement necessary and in this view a tree has flattened 10 cars that should not have been there as the ground is not surfaced. The Port of course were not liable, they never were, and our insurance company cancelled our policy as a result of this claim.

The Dutch mine sweeper navy viewed from **Olau Britannia** (2). One memorable night in November 1975 the **Olau Dana** broke her mooring lines in a storm and drifted into this wooden hulled flotilla crushing many of them. A crew member later told me that they were unaware of all the excitement whilst taking breakfast in the crew mess. The first she knew there was a problem was when a tug pushed out a porthole which landed in her Corn Flakes! The later Olau built ships all had strengthened pushing points for tugs which were clearly marked to avoid this kind of embarassment.

A close up of the damage to both bulkhead and cargo trailer aboard the m.v. **Argo.** The weight of a moving ship, even moving dead slow, creates tremendous inertia, and the most minor of collisions as in this case can twist steel like plasticine.

party liability arising from the ships' trading, ie the cargo, the passengers and any third party claim that may arise out of the ships trade.

Protection & Indemnity Insurance is placed with a P&I Club which is a mutual association rather than straight forward insurers. A mutual association is one formed of a group of shipping operators with similar risks. A managing agent is appointed and all operators put money into a general pot. Members claims are paid from this general pot in accordance with the terms of their entry in the Club and when a year closes there may be a call on members for a premium

adjustment or a surplus to roll into the next year or refund. Some club risks may be placed on the insurance market or just an excess insured.

Some time after the **Olau Finn** left we received a writ from the Post Office for £250,000. There are many techniques for berthing a ship but most depend on the power available to the Captain in terms of propellers and bow thrusters. Our old berth was not an easy berth and one method for berthing in a gale was to run past the berth, drop an anchor, and back onto the berth using the anchor to hold the bow firm. We did not know, up until we received the writ that is, that the Post Office had a telephone cable running from Sheerness to the Isle of Grain which the **Olau Finn** had been swinging on via its anchor. Our first indication was a writ and a cable laying ship off Sheerness making good the damage. One of the few advantages of running with chartered ships was that this type of litigation is for the account of the owner and his P&I Club. The writ was duly returned as Olau were not liable.

P&I Club liability has traditionally been unlimited but a number of clubs are now moving to restrict some types of claims such as pollution, (remember the **Exxon Valdez**) as the figures involved are becoming unmanageable. One other odd quirk about P&I Clubs is that all premiums are due on the 20th February in each year which is allegedly the day the ice is supposed to melt in the Baltic and trade can recommence. Ice in the Baltic no longer restricts trade as it did in the days of the Hanseatic League so this too will probably change with time.

Chapter 3

SHIPS

OPERATIONS

Everything about a ship is expensive, and whether Olau owned or chartered ships the actual daily running cost was virtually the same whether it ran or was laid up. These daily dead costs are known as demurrage and from a ship operator's point of view must be avoided at all costs. A ship must be kept working as many days of the year as physically possible to earn its keep.

A ship does however have one significant advantage in that, unlike a building, it is a floating asset, literally, it can be moved by its owners at will to a better trade if circumstances dictate.

The freight/car deck on a ship is like a car park, with our last ships a very big car park indeed. Into this 'car park' both passenger cars and freight customers from all over Europe booked space for a particular sailing. Some did not turn up (no-shows) and some turned up that had not booked (go-shows), but either way it was a mind blowing resource problem. Things were so tight that the actual margin of error was only 1.7 metres, equivalent to one small car on the car deck.

Our ships on arrival had to clear Customs, discharge both cargo and passengers, take stores, bunkers and fresh water if required, change some crew, carry out any maintenance, be cleaned and serviced, and then reloaded to sail on time. At Olau this was all achieved

A picture of demurrage. The **Olau Britannia** (2) is in dry dock in the Schelde Shipyard for attention to her bow thruster after having touched the bank in Vlissingen harbour and ingested a boulder. Unplanned dry-docking is doubly expensive as traffic has been booked on the ship and has to be re-routed, often to the opposition.

in four hours but sister ships in the Baltic in the summer did this in just over one hour!

The First Mate would start by supervising the unloading on arrival, then go to the freight office and passenger check-in for details of what was booked, in order to work out his deck space requirements and which of the hanging decks to use if any. This job

The upper car deck on **Olau Hollandia** (2). On this occasion it is literally a car park as a local Mazda dealership took it over for the launch of their new 1991 models.

A view of the old ferry terminal in April 1981 with **Olau Hollandia** (1) in the background. This was our first full ship as such and this view is from the top of one of the lighting towers, unfortunately loading is well advanced as I had hoped to capture a full vehicle park.

involved considerable skill as the ship also had to be trimmed. Furthermore some refrigerated vehicles would have to plug into the ship's power, which was only available at certain fixed points, disabled car passengers had to park by the lifts but most of all, the vehicles would not necessarily be available for loading as would be wished. Despite these obstacles the Company expected every inch of car deck to be used with nothing being left behind and the sailing schedule

to be maintained. It was enough to make a grown man cry as our computer had already calculated what would fit and we all know computers are never wrong!

Olau's day sailing times were set having regard to selling packages in London and Amsterdam, thus allowing passengers to have breakfast at their hotel before leaving to catch the ship. The night sailings were scheduled around passengers and freight drivers getting a night's rest before setting off the next day.

Three tugs of 'Knight's navy' now part of Alexander Tugs. These are **Kenley, Kennet and Keston**; each of these had one single but very large propeller and cost around £750 each for giving assistance either to berth or unberth. Knight's also had a 'super' tug with two propellers which could swivel and negated the need for a rudder. The 'Super tug' was worth two of the others in terms of power but of course cost twice as much as well.

The night sailings were longer for this reason although we lost an hour going east due to the time differential most of the year.

The Captains had to contend with all weathers of course, busy shipping lanes and particularly in the Thames, and Schelde estuaries, very strong tides (4 knots). In addition in the latter years the entrance to the North Edinburgh Channel in the Thames Estuary was becoming increasingly difficult to navigate at low tides as it was filling with sand.

The channels in the Thames Estuary were constantly moving around and were surveyed regularly by the River Department of the Port of Sheerness and the Port of London Authority. Nevertheless the timetable still had to be maintained but also with an eye to bunker consumption.

Our later ships were fitted with computer controlled economisers into which the timetable, and expected weather and tides were programmed. After sailing, the economisers would take over the engine management and switch engines in and out of line so as to arrive on time with optimum fuel consumption. We always said that if the ships sailed from Sheerness on the top of the tide it was literally downhill all the way to Holland.

Navigation is all done by satellite control these days and the ship's position can be pinpointed to within one second, ie one sixtieth of a nautical mile. A sextant was still carried onboard and calculating a position the 'old way' still formed part of the job with the younger keener officers doing it occasionally to keep their 'hands in'. One officer told me that some years ago in his deep sea days he had sailed in a ship from America to Australia with only a school atlas just by keeping the ship in mid ocean. Frightening is it not ?

Both the **Olau Hollandia** (I) and (2) and their sisters were fitted with controllable reversible pitch propellers, two enormous bow thrusters and two independent

Captain Peter Rodehache at the **Olau Britannia** (2)'s port console berthing the ship in Sheereness in May 1994.

rudders. These gave the ships considerable manoeuvring ability and avoided the use of tugs in all but extreme weather conditions.

The moment of greatest risk of damage to a ship is whilst berthing and unberthing. Touching the berth at anything over 0.5 knot risks damage to the berth or ship or both. In practice the trick is to stop and pull the ship in on the winches and line up the berthing markers on the ship and on shore. No two Captains were the same and each had their own particular ways of going about the same job.

Our Chief Executive remarked to me one day that prompt berthing indicated strong nerves not necessarily a better technique. Certainly I have seen the Captains on many occasions nonchalantly berth the ships in terrible weather as if they were parking a rowing boat. Watching, or rather, trying to watch the ships berth in fog was also amazing. Fog of course

The engine room control panel of **Olau Hollandia** (2).

means no wind and usually little tide but berthing a 160 metre ship by radar to an accuracy of half a metre when you cannot see your hand in front of your face is very impressive. Each to their own.

Oddly enough the greatest risk of all to a ship is not from the weather, or the sea but from fire. That is why considerable design work goes into fire control systems and fire fighting training on board ship. Olau's ships bristled with fire detectors which were all linked to a control panel on the bridge: in addition there were fire watchmen who constantly checked all decks. The problem with a ship fire is that it can rapidly transfer from one area to another along metal pipes, and wiring, where they are exposed to extreme heat. This is not always obvious as it happens between decks.

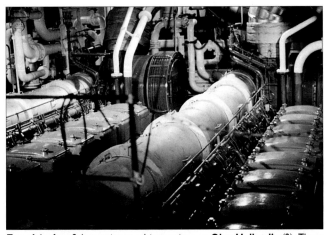

Two of the four Sulzer main propulsion engines on **Olau Hollandia** (2). These engines were the most expensive available at the time to fit but also the cheapest to operate as their fuel management engineering was more advanced which gave a one pay back on the additional capital cost

Modern ships incorporate many safety features to minimise this risk but the fact remains that the worst risk to a ship is from fire and not from the sea. Consequently all furnishings on board ship are made from fire retardant materials.

Engine rooms on ships, it was once said, are places for otherwise unemployable Scotsmen. Those days are now gone. No longer is the engine room like something from Dante's Inferno: today, as everywhere else, it is run by computers. Olau's last ships were driven by four Sulzer diesel engines driving through two gearboxes to the twin shafts. The pistons in these things were the size of large dustbins and the engine room itself when all four were running, was top of my list of places to avoid. It was strictly an ear muff and hard hat area as the noise had nowhere to go and seemed to bounce around for ever trying desperately to get out. The engines themselves took up two decks.

Olau's route took it over a number of shallow sand banks and about once a year the engine water jackets had to be stripped down to remove the enormous mussels that had got through the filters. These intrepid crustaceans had, when small, found a nice safe place to live with a constant supply of flowing water and of course a regular supply of food. The ships' chefs looked forward with relish to this aspect of the ships' maintenance.

LAUNCHES & DRY-DOCKING

Olau, in its brief lifetime, built four ships for its own use, the first **Olau Hollandia** and **Olau Britannia** at 14,550 tons in 1980 and 1981 and the second larger versions at 35,000 tons in 1989 and 1990 respectively.

All Olau's ships were built at AG Weser, now Seebeckwerft in Bremerhaven. The ships followed a

Olau Hollandia (2) prior to official naming, and launching on the ways at A G Weser's shipyard Bremerhaven in November 1980. This ship took six months from the first plate being laid to launching. The yard is paid in progress payments as various pre-specified works in the contract are completed and the yard men are on corresponding related bonuses.

basic TT Line tried and tested concept for use on their services in the Baltic. For many years Baltic ferries have been streets ahead in interior standards compared with those plying from the UK. This was in part was due to the high standards of living prevailing in all countries adjoining the Baltic Sea and virtual prohibition in Sweden. The Baltic has an additional advantage of little or no tide, and being an inland sea, does

The builder's plate on **Olau Hollandia** (1). Builder's number 1028. This plate was fitted to the wall at Information, with very long permanent bolts to deter souvenir hunters.

not experience regular rough weather as can quickly appear in the Channel. It does, however, freeze over in winter close to land.

Seebeckwerft, had a long association of building ships for TT Line and Olau became the beneficiary of this experience. The first two Olau ships took an incredible 10 months to build from the first plates being laid until delivery. These ships had very large cabin

Olau Britannia (1) was launched in December 1981. The weather was bitterly cold and sleet the size of golf balls was falling. My light meter would barely read during the usual long speeches but literally minutes before launching the weather cleared to sunshine and a blue sky.

The **Olau Britannia** (1) takes to the water safely and is nursed by tugs to the fitting out berth. Within minutes the weather closed in again to a Stygian gloom and we had had the best of the day, about five minutes. I remember being really impressed as to how well connected our shareholders must have been.

An aerial view of Seebeckwerft's yard in Bremerhaven in August 1989. **Olau Britannia** (2), builders' No 1068 is on the ways to be launched on 28th October 1989. (Olau collection)

accommodation, most with en suite facilities which was unheard of way back in 1980. The world was changing, and we at Olau sensing the mood wanted to pre-empt the change.

The slipways at Seebeckwerft are like the two forks of a letter 'Y' where the fork are the two slips and the central stem the basin into which they lead. All Olau ships were built on the right hand 'Y' and launches were interesting as the ship had to enter the water and then twist to the right, sorry starboard, and of course stop. This was achieved by attaching a 100 ton concrete block on the starboard side and a 50 ton block on the port side via an anchor chain rather than the traditional drag chains which now seem to have gone out of fashion. Tugs waited in the basin to receive the ship and nurse her to a fitting out berth.

All launches were like a main event in Bremerhaven which is no doubt how it was on Tyneside and in Glasgow when the UK was the workshop of the British

Captain Mantei, Captain Bohn and Heinz Kerstan, Managing Director of Olau Line at the hand over and Christening of **Olau Hollandia** (2). The lectern, which belongs to the shipyard acquired a new Christening plate as each new ship is delivered.

Olau Britannia (2) at her fitting out berth at Lloydswerft, Bremerhaven. (Olau Collection)

Case Rietkerk chats with Graeme Dunlop and Les Stevenson of P&O European Ferries at the Christening of **Olau Hollandia** (2).

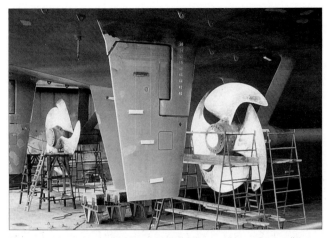

The two independent rudders and controllable reversible pitch propellers on **Olau Hollandia** (2) The light strips are sacrificial anodes to limit the corrosive effect of the sea. (Olau collection)

The launch of **Olau Hollandia** (2) and the moment of impact with the dock wall. (Olau collection)

The author (5'8") giving an impression of scale to the **Olau Hollandia** (2)'s port propeller. Shipyards are a definite hard hat area but as one of my colleagues pointed out, if the ship had fallen on my head I would not need a hard hat, just a box !

The bulbous bow of **Olau Hollandia** (2). This was not for ice breaking but acted as a stabiliser holding the ship level in the water. Behind the bulbous bow are the bow thruster tunnels with a water pressure relief tunnel in the middle. Note that the bow visor had not yet been cut out, this was done when the ship took to the water as the stresses had all changed. (Olau collection)

The disco on **Olau Hollandia** (2) - four days before the ship was due to be delivered !

Chief Officer Manfred Boss on board **Olau Hollandia** (2) in Lloydswerft at Bremerhaven. I have just asked him if he thinks the ship will be finished for our press trip in four days time.

Empire. The yard opened its gates and it seemed like everyone in the world had come to watch; Bremerhaven after all was a shipyard town and many businesses relied for their livelihood on the sea.

The first Olau ships were built in the early 80's at a time when UK yards were in stop go mode; I particularly recall the tremendous sense of justifiable

National pride at Bremerhaven when the German National Anthem was played prior to a launch. Everyone stood to attention in absolute silence, followed by that awesome 'crack' noise as the last chock was pressed out by a hydraulic jack and the ship started to move for the first time.

out. In practice a number of shipyard workers usually stayed on board to finish off but they always kept out of sight of everyone.

After fitting-out come the sea trials where the shipyard Captain puts the ship through its paces in the presence of the owner's Marine Superintendents, and

An aerial view of the **Olau Finn** at Oslo Quay Hamburg in the dry-dock of Howaldtswerke-Deuthsche Werft for its annual inspection. (Olau collection)

Olau Britannia (2) having its hull pressure-cleaned at the Schelde Shipyard in May 1993.

The **Olau Britannia** (2) in emergency dry-docking for repairs to its bow thruster.

The second generation of Olau ships were physically too big for the slipway as they actually hit the corner of the dock during launching. This was one of those odd situations whereby it was better for the shipyard to have the work and repair the damage than not have the work at all.

Fitting out is absolute mayhem particularly in the last few days. Literally hundreds of sub contractors are crawling all over the ship completing their particular job. It was both worrying and impressive to watch. In the end, however it was like having a house built, you move in on a certain day to make the builders move

the new Ships Master and Chief Engineer. This involves testing everything to the limit, maximum speed, stopping time, turning, manoeuvring and of course all the onboard safety equipment. This is normally done with the army of subcontractors still on board and the ship then returns to the fitting out basin for final completion. **Olau Hollandia** (I) on her sea trials was able to do a crash stop from full speed of 23 knots in three times her own length.

The next stage is the official hand over from the shipyard to the new owners. This, at Olau was normally done during a small cruise with press and dignitaries onboard. The shipyard Captain took the ship out into Heligoland Bight and the ship was stopped in the water. Various, usually long, speeches, preceded the lowering of the shipyard flag and the raising of the new owners' flag. This is followed by numerous toasts followed by everyone with any sense rushing inside in the warm for a celebration luncheon.

It is only following the hand-over that the owners' Captain and Chief Engineer actually get 'hands on' experience of the ship although both have been present at the yard since the first plate was laid to oversee the owners' requirements.

Dry-docking was always a stressful time for all concerned whether planned or otherwise. The most economical time to dry-dock our ships was January or February when both passenger and freight traffic was low but much of the external work carried out at this time of the year was of limited value. Ships accumulate a layer of algae below the water line whilst in service and once a year this has to be cleaned off or it actually slows the ship down and increases bunker consumption in the end.

Once this algae is cleaned off, the ship is surveyed and the hull repainted. Cleaning is normally by means of high pressure water jets which in winter tended to replace the slime with a layer of ice. Even if paint could be applied in such temperatures it usually would not dry in a lasting manner.

With the **Olau Kent** we actually tried for a while to clean the underside of the ship whilst in port at Vlissingen during turn round by means of a remote magnetic limpet scrubbing machine. However as nobody has yet invented underwater paint this exercise was of limited value.

Whilst in dry dock all the other underwater parts such as propellers, bow thrusters, rudders and stabilisers also receive attention as required and we always all prayed that the shafts did not have to be drawn. Drawing of propeller shafts normally means trouble with a capital T. Not only is it a time consuming and delicate exercise but you never know what you will find. Remedial work in this area was normally expensive, and on occasions only temporary, whilst spares were manufactured with further dry-docking required to fit them.

Normal scheduled dry-docking is booked months in advance with the first dry-dock session after delivery normally at the builder's yard. Although at Olau we lost two days demurrage on this returning to Bremerhaven, it paid for itself in avoiding having to claim any defect work via an intermediate ship yard. Later dry-dockings were normally done in the Schelde shipyard just east of Vlissingen.

Before the ship arrives at the dry-dock, graving or floating, large keel blocks have to be laid out to take the ship's weight. The ship is pulled into the dock by capstans whilst tugs hold the stern straight. The weather has to be relatively favourable for this exercise, or more demurrage ensues. However 'sods law' dictated it always seemed to blow like hell on the day the ship was due out so experience taught us to not take any new bookings for the 'first' sailing until we knew the ship was actually out and on its way.

The key in the end to running a reliable service is good maintenance and at Olau this was always the order of the day. Maintenance is a prerequisite to running a reliable service and it also maintains the resale value of the ship.

Olau built four ships for its own use over the years and for the benefit of those who do not know the difference between a boat and a ship, boats are carried on ships.

Olau Britannia (2) in the Schelde Shipyard floating dry-dock.

Part of the Captain's Buffet on board **Olau Britannia (2).**

ON BOARD SERVICE

From the first sailing Ole Lauritzen wanted something new, something different, and most of all to be the best. What the original **Olau East** and **Olau West** lacked in creature comforts, cabins, etc was made up for in service. Danish service and Danish cuisine.

Running a ferry business is not just a matter of selling a ticket for a passenger or freight passage. Olau had a seven to nine hour crossing which meant that accommodation, food and entertainment had to be provided. We started with entertainment on the **Olau East** and the **Olau West** as a disco but this matured with the introduction of the first **Olau Hollandia** and **Olau Britannia** into live bands and on the second generation ships a cabaret as well.

The costs of running the ships was enormous and everything we did in a small or big way helped to defray these costs so that hopefully in the end we made a profit. Contributions to profit came from all directions apart from sea freight and fares, but also from the terminal kiosk and telephone franchises ashore, to currency exchange, luggage storage, gaming on board, food, drink and of course duty free and gifts.

The major contributor apart from the basic passage fare and catering came from duty free sales which was almost a licence to print money. The cost to Olau of a normal litre bottle of scotch, duty free, in 1994 was £2.10 which would sell for £9.50 still a substantial saving on the Tesco price. Cigarettes are after all only old leaves and rice paper with most of the cost of a pack of 200 being in the packaging; a pack of 200 filter would cost around £1.00 duty free and sell happily at £12.

This explains how the short sea routes could dump their fares at a £1 a passenger; their ships could do several round trips a day with the possibility to sell duty free each time and in each direction. Olau did not reduce its fares and could only sell duty free, with its longer crossing, twice in every 24 hours against up to 10 times on the short sea routes. It followed therefore that our fare structure could not be and was not supported by duty free sales although what we did sell was profitable.

Duty Free has its origins going back several hundred years. One theory is that in the 17th and 18th centuries the landed gentry of England would push their offspring through private school and university much as happens today. However on completing their education and these early day Hooray Henrys would be sent on a Grand Tour of Europe visiting each of the principal cities in turn to gain a classical world wise education before returning to the family pile to run the estate. Because of the perceived difficulty of obtaining one's preferred malt in the then Capitals of Europe a suitable supply to sustain the trip, which could be several years, was allowed to such travellers Duty Free.

According to the Duty Free Federation however the concession started as a travellers' allowance applicable specifically to ships which were generally considered Stateless for duty purposes. Ships would put into port and generally be allowed to purchase supplies of the local

An Olau menu card

29

A general view of the main restaurant onboard **Olau Hollandia** (2).

hooch 'tax free' on the basis that they were for export or would be consumed in International waters. This was an informal arrangement until ratified in 1944 by the Chicago Convention which officially created duty free. The actual allowances as such were set in 1954 when air travel became more common, and these allowances have remained much the same ever since. It was and is today a traveller's allowance.

There is however an argument that goes if you neither smoke nor drink (ie do not buy any duty free ever, even for someone else) then your fare is being subsidised by those that do.

The trick of course is to pitch a retail price that is attractive to all your passengers in Olau's case Dutch, German, Danish and English. This is not easy as despite the EC and for a short while the ERM, tariffs do differ between EC member states as do retail prices. At Olau we found it very difficult to find levels of prices that would catch all, most were a best option whilst maximising profit.

Food on board was another problem as we were catering for many Nationalities but mainly Dutch (35%),

Captain Mantei and the main restaurant catering staff aboard **Olau Hollandia** (2).

The roulette and blackjack room on **Olau Britannia** (2) before closure. These facilities were popular with both the Company for providing a lucrative profit contribution and passengers as a welcome distraction to pass the time. A freight driver once won £6000 on one of our tables on the **Olau Kent** way back in 1977 but without winners there are no losers, and as word got round of this big win we quickly recouped this loss many times over. (Olau collection)

English (45%) German (15%) Danish and others (5%). On the continent for example they like their meat on the hoof (swimming in blood) and whilst this did not bother me most Brits would go hysterical at this. The continentals also loved raw herrings which were a speciality on board with many different variations included in the Captain's Buffet. The minute a Brit knew the fish was raw, that was it and certainly opening a herring bar would be the quickest way to go broke in the UK.

Our menus therefore were a minefield for the catering manager and passenger alike, an honest attempt to please all, that sometimes pleased nobody. (We all know someone who only eats burger, beans and chips on holiday and avoids that foreign muck).

In the last days of Olau, flambé (in calm weather) was added to the menu options although the waiter had to stand clear of the many fire detectors in the restaurant. This was an instant success which was denied the opportunity of further development.

The second generation **Olau Hollandia** and **Olau Britannia** represented the epitome of passenger ferry design and on board service but for Olau the storm clouds were already brewing. The ships represented an enormous investment (£55 million each) and were introduced under the second German register which allowed a certain proportion of non EC crew.

A major problem arose first with the gaming on board which was franchised to an independent company. The problem was that the ships were registered in Hamburg and a gaming licence had to be granted by the City of Hamburg but these were strictly limited in number. The actual licences, as often happens where gambling is involved, were already well sewn up by others. Despite the fact that we never sailed near Hamburg we were denied a gaming licence and ordered to close our casino and gaming machines

immediately.

There were problems elsewhere as well. Unfortunately the Seebetriebsrat (German workers' council) decided on opening times of shops and onboard facilities to the extent that most were never properly utilised. It was a tragedy that such luxurious ships were never able to reach their full potential with Olau. It is interesting now to note that with our ships, P&O have the facilities open 24 hours a day, something we could only dream of thanks to the Seebetriebsrat.

Without the opportunity for gaming, ridiculous work practice restrictions and abuses, Olau was thereby denied the opportunity to exploit the ships' five star facilities to the full.

From 1991 onwards our ships were run for the convenience of some of the crew, rather than the passengers and shareholders. Olau's fate was effectively sealed.

The ship's notice from onboard setting out the opening and closing times of the facilities.

Chapter 4

TRADING WITH OLAU

PASSENGER TRAFFIC

Olau's target market was the highest revenue generating passengers for all its sailings, but inevitably there was a large shortfall in Olau's case, and probably everyone else's as well, on mid-week sailings. The reason for this is that many people are forced to take their holidays in blocks of one week, weekend to weekend, or are tied to school holidays.

We did however have one advantage at Olau in that we were able to take full benefit of most of the holiday periods as very few English, Dutch and German holidays actually overlapped beyond the obvious Christmas Day and Easter Sunday breaks.

Ideally we wanted car drivers with 4 passengers although the average actually was nearer to 2.2 due to business travellers. Following the Gulf War we picked up a lot of new business traffic and what is more kept it. Many Companies at that time would not allow their key senior executives to fly at this time for the fear of terrorism so this traffic naturally went to the ferries. At Olau there were no such restrictions on managers flying and I for one was never sure if we were not designated as key senior executives or merely just regarded as dispensable.

Although we had a rail link into Sheerness via a branch line from Sittingbourne which was on the London-Dover main line, we never reached any significant volumes of 'classic' passengers, the trade designation for rail foot passengers travelling on through tickets. In the circumstances we ran a bus service to London instead that dropped off at the hotels used in our packages sold abroad.

Initially when British Rail (BR) owned Sealink, BR protected Sealink's patch like a mother hen and always evaded giving us ITX rates (inclusive fares) which may compete in any way. Instead we were stuck with rack rates, less 10% commission, although they did condescend to our holding ticket stocks in

Mad dogs and Englishmen go out in the mid day sun. Many people were caught out by the combination of sun, a sea breeze and heat reflected from steel. On board ship was a great place for a quick sun tan. From Olau's point of view this type of weather was good for the pictures in the brochure but bad for business as everyone went on deck and tended to stay there. The ideal weather for on board spend was a calm sea with either, rain or a cold wind outside or, even better, both.

exchange for a bond. The Sealink and BR people were always sniffing round in the early days in their dress uniform of the day of bowler hat, black jacket and pin striped trousers. These visits were always on the pretext of giving us ITX rates but were actually just an excuse to be inquisitive. On our part we were flattered by their attention and usually got a free lunch.

All this changed with the privatisation of Sealink which was bought from the Government as I recall for only £64 million. Suddenly freed from the Sealink tacit interference, BR were all over us like a rash and in no time we were able to offer through fares from London to Amsterdam and other destinations at competitive rates. From then we enjoyed a fruitful relationship until our closure in May 1994 although the classic passenger became more and more the rucksack brigade (students) and as such did not fall into our market profile.

The remaining part of our passenger business came from tour operators who organised their own package of which the ferry crossing was a component part. This market is extremely competitive and has changed out of all recognition over the years.

From Olau's point of view a tour operator could offer a bus load of people, perhaps on a low sailing up to 52 weeks a year and as such could enjoy a discount on our group rates. This however involved a kind of chicken and egg scenario. The tour operator needed good rates from all his component suppliers in order to market a particular trip at a competitive price. This effectively meant we had to offer a discount on anticipated income, and invariably found the tour operator had been over optimistic.

In 1976 Europe was crawling with Americans and at Olau we had our fair share. These were top notch passengers as they always seemed to have too much money to spend and part of our equation in assessing a passenger group rate is the on board spend per

The Helsinki-registered **Olau Finn** en route to Vlissingen shortly after entering service in May 1976. (Fotoflite)

Olau West. (Fotoflite)

passenger. (Scouts for example would be a low onboard spend).

However since the late 80's our share of the American market has declined in line I believe with European trends. More and more Americans it seems were holidaying at home. We put this down to fear of terrorism, the early 80's were all hi-jackings and suicide bombers mostly targeted against Americans abroad either as tourists or military. It was easy to play Rambo from a safe distance of 5000 miles but none of them it seemed wanted an unscheduled stopover in Beirut.

When our first two bespoke ships arrived in the early 80's we were able to fully tap the group market as for the first time we were able to offer, indeed guarantee, cabin accommodation on night sailings. The traditional coach market at that time, oddly enough, came from the Midlands, the North West and Scotland being mainly middle aged to elderly couples who had grown up children and wanted to start taking quick breaks. These type of passengers are irreverently known as 'wrinklies' in the trade.

Our relationship with the tour operators however was not always a bed of roses. Many thought we gave 3 months credit, despite what the contract said, and one or two abused the right of holding ticket stocks by writing out tickets for what they had requested and not what was confirmed. On balance though it all seemed to work well until the late 80's when their traditional markets just evaporated away. We then shifted our strategy to dealing, indeed targeting, the much smaller coach operator who paid a better rate, only ran a few trips a year and were less demanding.

The 1990's saw a new breed of coach operator running the new generation of super coaches. The comparatively few large operators that remained, following a spate of failures, were being quoted what we regarded as silly rates by our competitors and Olau was not prepared to buy business. We did however on several occasions undercut other ferry operators, not to get the business, but to make them the opposition come underneath us to keep it. This was out of curiosity to see how far they would go. The answer was all the way, keep the business at any price.

Olau as a ferry service was deliberately not cheap. We were offering something different, something better for the discerning passenger who had a choice and wanted to be treated as a person. Travelling in the 1930's was like that, and it was not necessarily a paradise lost. On the voyage to India, the rule then was port out starboard home, to stay on the cool side of the ship, which of course no longer applied as our ships were fully air conditioned throughout.

Our two generations of new ships were each licensed to carry 1600 passengers but this could easily have been uplifted to 2000-2200 subject to additional lifesaving equipment. In truth we did not want this, we only had a few sailings a year where we booked to the 1600 maximum in any case but we more than anything wanted people to have space to move and be able to relax.

Olau also had its fare share of passengers on a one way trip to their maker either by suicide, stupidity or just passing away peacefully. This was always a depressing and upsetting business for all directly involved. It happened that in one week alone we had two deaths and then suddenly had our first birth which made everyone's day. A young lady, who was great with child, in the Biblical sense, decided to dance the night away in the ship's Disco on the **Olau Hollandia** (2)

Holland is made up of many Islands joined together by bridges and dykes. Vlissingen is on the Island of Walcheren on the north bank of the Schelde estuary but there is also a small part of Holland adjoining Belgium on the south side with a ferry port at Breskens. In this view **Olau Hollandia** (1) is turning into Vlissingen harbour whilst the Breskens Ferry slips out behind her. When Olau started its service from Vlissingen the Dutch diverted the motorway virtually into the Port. In England though it was a different story; in Holland they anticipate demand and put in the infrastructure whilst in England we always seem to run along behind with road schemes for yesterday.

Lifeboat drill for all crew was a compulsory part of the ship's routine together with fire fighting drill. In this view of a drill in Sheerness one of the boats is lowered from **Olau Hollandia** (2). The lifeboats were rotated with each drill to ensure they were all kept in working order.

which proved to be not a good idea. Her baby was delivered in the ship's hospital by an army surgeon travelling as a passenger and it made everyone onboard feel good. It was a first, and a pleasant change.

There is an old tradition for babies born on a ship to also have the Christening on board using the ship's bell as a font. This went back to the days of mass emigration to Australia where many children were born on the six week voyage. As the child mortality rate was high in those days babies were immediately Christened using the inverted ship's bell. We felt this would be a good first, but it was not to be as our letters offering the ship's facilities for a Christening and reception all went unanswered. None of our staff who were expecting were too keen on volunteering to give birth on board either so we never did get to revive this old tradition.

Another thing that was different about Olau is that we would not carry football groups knowingly neither did we encourage all-male groups. As a private Company we were not a 'common carrier' by law which meant we could actually make a choice if we so wished. British Rail on the other hand is a 'common carrier' and has to carry anyone who can afford a ticket provided he or she abides by their voluminous byelaws.

We were more selective and always quizzed tour operators about groups that were booked on or around overseas football fixtures, receiving some very imaginative replies, such as pilgrims, brass rubbing group, works outing etc. If we were in any doubt we asked for a bond from the tour operator; this normally helped the tour operator focus his mind, if he was in

any doubt, and dubious bookings would promptly cancel and re-book with a less discerning short sea operator.

Our thinking was obvious, we were in a different market, and with a seven hour crossing, groups could get very drunk in that time. Certainly we had no all male groups that sat and read from the Bible all the way across. The short sea routes only have them for between one to two hours so there is a limit to the drink that can be consumed. Although Olau provided on board security, tackling a bus load of drunks was not a practical proposition so we would not let anyone onboard ship to start with if they arrived drunk.

We usually allowed football supporters travelling to a game by car to travel as they tended to be cut from different cloth, but we always reserved the right to refuse them if circumstances so dictated.

Our cells sadly saw regular use, particularly on a Friday and Saturday night. There was usually at least one passenger who managed to get himself silly and was locked up, often as much for his own protection, invariably to be refused landing on the other side and deported back. I once enquired if these cells had heating, 'of course', was the answer, 'in the summer we have it on and in the winter we have it off !'

It sometimes seemed strange to us that whilst the other ferries from Ramsgate and Dover were literally dumping their passenger fares (£1 a passenger) we were still as busy as ever on a sensible fare structure. From this it would be easy to conclude that is why they are still around and we are not: perhaps there is something we have missed. I am sure though it is not as straight forward as that.

PACKAGE HOLIDAYS

When Olau started its ferry service in 1974 the question of package holidays could not be further from our minds but very quickly, given the demand, they became a logical extension of our operation for the most obvious of reasons. As the ferry business developed we received more and more requests from passengers for us to find them a hotel in Holland, usually for their first night's stay, but people often wanted more. Of course we were happy to oblige and from this initial demand a small hotel booking service grew up.

We soon found that what had started as an additional free customer service rapidly expanded into all kinds of packages from hotels to bungalow parks and bargain breaks to round trips; indeed we even tried, albeit briefly, putting together ski packages but this was ill-fated and short-lived.

It is interesting to note retrospectively how our market changed over the years. We started with hotels, expanded into bungalow parks and returned in the later years to hotel bargain breaks which were by far the most popular in our latter years. We of course added refinements such as entertainment, bicycle hire, speciality meals and entrance vouchers but all were based around the ship and if possible targeting low sailings.

The eighties saw our best passenger carryings on packages ever but from that point they went into a

An impressive view of the **Olau Kent** on her 7 hour crossing to Sheerness. (Fotoflite)

The **Olau Hollandia** (1) off the Kentish coast en-route to Holland. (Fotoflite)

Double vision? The first and second **Olau Hollandia** (of 1981 and 1989) at Sheerness together on 3rd October 1989. The older ship leaves on her penultimate voyage while the new vessel lies at the new linkspan on her first visit to the Kentish port. (Fotoflite)

An early Olau poster quoting Dr. Samuel Johnson. Ever a wit Dr. Johnson also said, "being in a ship, is like being in jail, with the chance of being drowned". This illustrates the importance of choosing the right caption for a poster.

trailer. Although we offered packages in this market, availability was deliberately restricted and low sailings targeted. Caravans and car trailers take up valuable deck space, are normally low revenue earning and caravans particularly damage easily if the driver is not completely competent at manoeuvring. Although any damage would be down to the driver it was unnecessary aggravation.

In fact Olau's target market of Social Economic Group ABCI's did not necessarily include those with caravans and we generally tended to leave this market for the pile it high and sell it cheap short sea routes.

It is interesting to reflect on how the travel world has changed in the past twenty years and people's aspirations with it. When Olau started we often carried full ships on night sailings when there were only berths for several hundred. Passengers were quite happy to sleep on the floor, under stairs, in seats, on coat hangers indeed anywhere and what is more people were prepared to share cabins with strangers.

From the mid eighties onwards we found our night capacity was limited to cabin availability with passengers prepared to buy cabins for sole use at full price rather than share. Curiously where cabin sharing was involved, all passengers tended to be xenophobic. If they had to share, and most preferred not to, it must be with one of their own countrymen.

The whole business of running a holiday department however was very expensive and as our market share declined a radical rethink became necessary. Our brochure was running to 32 pages, much of it for package holidays whilst the cost of servicing the packages, booking, confirmation, payment and vouchers was tedious, time consuming and labour intensive. We had very few allocations as such so each hotel had to be faxed for availability whilst the client was put on hold. Once confirmation and payment were received the ticket and vouchers were despatched; about one in four however came back for minor

steady decline in the 1990's. The world had changed again, bungalow parks were no longer in vogue and cheaper air packages with guaranteed wall to wall sunshine were taking over. Although the drive holiday, Olau's traditional market, still existed, we found ourselves in the second holiday market rather than the main holiday and adjusted our sales strategy accordingly.

The other type of package we offered was the camping holiday for those with either a caravan or tent

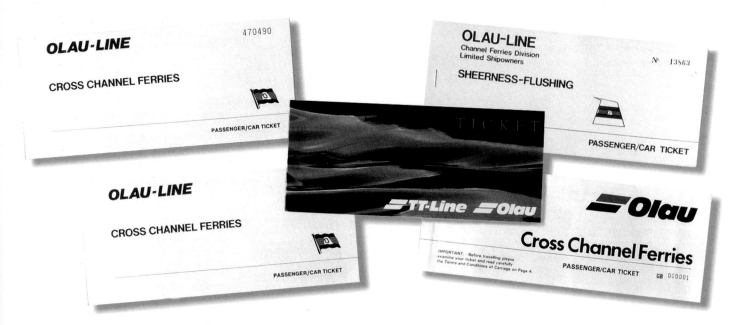

The evolution of Olau's passenger ticket, from cradle to the grave. A considerable time was spent on designing a user friendly ticket which, was easy to complete and easy to read. It is perhaps a shame that the ferries have not evolved a standard universal ticket with just a validation box for the operators logo as the International Airlines Travel Association (IATA) have developed for their member airlines.

Olau's first and last brochures. The last one was a thinking man's brochure as the design was based on the work of the Dutch artist Piet Mondrian, as 1994 being 50 years after his death special events were planned in Holland.

adjustment because 'Auntie could no longer come on that day' and the whole circus was repeated. We later introduced an amendment fee on all bookings which was discretionary but activated in certain circumstances; the record number of amendments on one booking was eight as I recall.

More recently the package holiday business has been burdened with new legislation from Brussels known as the EC Package Holiday Directive. As is usual with EC legislation in Britain we get on with applying it whilst in Holland and Germany they are rather more laid back and adopt the 'why do today what you can do tomorrow' approach.

There were two nasties in this legislation - one good and one bad. The first clause made us, as the tour operator within the terms of the directive, responsible for up to £5,000 worth of assistance to any passenger on a package who has a misfortune through no fault of his own. We assumed this to be something like one of our passengers getting knocked down by a bus and having no insurance of their own. This was buried in our terms and conditions to comply with the directive and we thought it would only be a matter of time before someone gave us a run on it. Meanwhile I had persuaded our nervous insurers to tack this onerous risk on the back of our Public Liability Insurance policy initially on a suck it and see basis. Although we had no claims under this obligation, other tour operators did, so our insurers got cold feet and from year two it became a separate risk carrying its own premium.

The other nasty, which is much more sensible, is the directive that allows a passenger to sue the tour operator in respect of any loss or injury suffered whilst on holiday in respect of component parts that make up the package. This means that if a passenger, on an Olau holiday, fell down stairs at one of the hotels in our brochure as, say the carpet was loose, they could sue Olau instead of the Dutch or German Hotelier. On our part we were required to inspect all hotels on offer and verify all facilities to ensure accurate descriptions

in our brochure plus check hoteliers insurances and fire certificates.

Olau at the beginning of 1991 offered some 300 plus hotels, many as so called Go-as-you-please but on the volumes we were booking, verification on such a scale made no sense at all. We therefore went in the opposite direction and consolidated what we were doing ending up in 1994 with relatively few actual packages and running a hotel booking service only. The wheel had turned a full circle, we were back where we started but what we did offer was manageable for our Vlissingen office to keep an eye on, was profitable and made sense in the market we now found ourselves.

Ironically at our demise we were experiencing a bumper year, much of which had to be re-booked with other ferry operators. Again under the package holiday directive, once we had accepted a booking we were obliged to make alternative arrangements if the passengers involved did not want a refund.

The moral of this story, if there is a moral, is that in the future only larger operators will be able to offer package holidays and afford to comply completely with the EC package holiday directive verification requirements. The alternative of course is not to bother and defend any litigation as it comes. In the end I see the package holiday market being dominated by the larger operators as only the high volume people can do this properly.

SEA FREIGHT

Freight, as every ferry operator knows is the vital mainstay of the business and it was freight that the experts suggested to Ole Lauritzen would be where the potential lay for a Sheerness to Vlissingen route. The service started in November 1974 with the chartered 1,877 ton m.v. **Basto V**. As a fledgling Company, newcomers indeed upstarts on the scene, we were initially the beneficiaries of all the hauliers that the other ferries did not want. These were exciting and dangerous times both financially and for some of us physically resulting in considerable bad debts. Fortunately however we also had some very good customers as well, who were by far in the majority and without whose continued support there is no doubt we could not have survived.

The early days were rough and tough, with Olau having to wind up on average, one freight Company every month. In doing this we came across some very colourful characters. It was common, but totally outrageous, for a haulier to come to see us pleading poverty, whilst dripping in gold medallions, diamond cuff links, and wearing £1000 suits. In those days the so-called matchbox trick was rife throughout the country, not just in the haulage industry.

For the uninitiated, or those who have led a sheltered life, the matchbox trick involves running a company to provide the directors with a living rather than to make a profit. Trade is obtained, and debts run up after a short while faster than the money is being earned. Bills are always paid promptly, to start with, but gradually they slip until a creditor 'pushes the button' and winds them up. Any leasing companies are

The launch of the new **Olau Britannia** (2) at Bremerhaven on the 28th October 1989. (Ferry Publications Library)

The **Olau Hollandia** (2) in the final stages of fitting out in Germany. (Ferry Publications Library)

usually quite affable about transferring any agreements to a new company and often property leases are transferred as well. Any real assets such as freeholds are normally outside the matchbox company.

On liquidation the company's name is changed to Going-broke Ltd or some such nonsense and a new company formed called Off-the-peg Ltd. Off-the-peg Ltd then changes its name to the original company name of the one that was scuttled and the only visible sign to the outside world is the change of Company registration number on the note paper. In all other respects it is business as usual. It was a lot easier than robbing a bank and it was legal, then.

This is also known as the 'long term fraud' although long term is normally only three to five years. The new Companies Acts specifically target this type of racket and Directors can be disqualified from holding office in certain circumstances. After a hesitant start this is now happening so the fraudsters move on to use their wives, relatives or goldfish as stooges, or just ignore the law. With computer databases though in the hands of Banks and Companies House, this type of fraud is happily on the decline at last.

On one memorable occasion Case Rietkerk and I saw two particular individuals who were built like an American tag team. Both had flattened noses, cauliflower ears, necks that merged into heads and sports jackets that were one size too small. The larger of the two, and both were very large, introduced

Olau's first sticker which came in three sizes, small medium and very large (2' diameter). Sheppey was so excited at the prospect of having its own ferry that these appeared on everything that moved in Sheerness and many things that did not; like street furniture etc.

himself , "Ello my name is Mr Smiff and this is my accountant Mr Jones" (names changed to protect the author). Outside was the obligatory white Mercedes with the engine running parked in the middle of our coach park. A large minder in dark glasses with black gloves leaned against the driver's door trying to smoke inconspicuously whilst looking around nervously like a cornered animal.

The meeting finished amiably, Case and I did not need hospital treatment, and we actually got some of the money we were owed before the serious crime squad caught up with Mr Smith & Mr Jones. They were it seemed running a racket of stealing goods vehicles, taking them abroad, usually to Turkey, selling the loads and then 'finding' the vehicles. They would then contact the insurer or rental company and get a reward for bringing them back, having first obtained from the owner some cash up front towards their repatriation expenses.

On another occasion I had to explain to three heavies early one morning why they could not have a

Freight lined up for loading in the winter of 1985. Most of these are 'accompanied' but the unit on the right is a 'road train'.

trailer we had impounded against overdue sea freight. They colourfully explained my life story but fortunately a couple of our larger stevedores chose that moment to come into the freight office. Once again I escaped having to eat hospital food. I mentioned this incident later to our Danish freight manager who suggested I should have told them I was only the cleaner! He said he would have done so, as cowards ran in his family.

Hauling goods to or from the continent in those days was quite complicated, expensive and time consuming. The margins then as now were small, and much effort was required for even a small profit. The older established companies who owned their own rigs were best placed, but nevertheless many of the smaller operators somehow survived and made a good living to boot.

Firstly you needed a rig, the most common being a tractor and trailer totalling 15 metres in length. We called these an 'accompanied' as they came accompanied by one or two big hairy lorry drivers, usually with hands like a bunch of bananas. A rig could cost anything from £20,000-£100,000 and may or may not include a refrigeration unit. As with a ship the rig then had to work to earn its keep, so the wheels had to keep turning.

Then you needed permits. Various EC countries allocated at that time permits for heavy goods vehicles to cross their borders on a one for one basis ie a UK lorry on their roads for one of theirs on ours. In a liquidation situation it was often the 'permits' that were a failed company's most valuable assets most of which had 'lapsed' or 'disappeared' long before any liquidator got in.

Freight movements in the 1970's were a quagmire of paperwork with various types of 'T' forms (transit documents) being required for the goods, Port Health examinations, Customs examinations, and bonding requirements for any duty payable on the goods.

Most hauliers used an agent, preferably one with a duty deferment account, to clear their goods. When our ship arrived and the ship's bag came ashore with the transit documents for the freight onboard, those agents who entered their client's paperwork first at the Customs EPU (Entry Process Unit) would clear Customs first. Time was literally money. Often more haste and less speed prevailed, and once Customs spotted an error or query, the documents were thrown out for amendment, and went to the bottom of the pack.

This situation gave birth to a freight agents' mini Le Mans getaway from the ferry terminal, first to the agents' portacabin or office and then to the EPU. The more enthusiastic agents had a driver with the car door open and engine running for this exercise and as a result many agents received warnings for dangerous driving in the docks which had a 20 mph speed limit. I

The **Olau Kent** leaving the pool of London to visit Liverpool and Glasgow before taking up service in March 1976. The ship was purchased from Viking Line and at this point in time still sported their red hull, this was replaced with Olau blue before entering service. (Olau collection)

personally was never sure if this was a minimum or maximum but somehow it all worked and thankfully nobody got hurt.

Customs clearance could take anything from 30 minutes to several days and the haulier also ran the risk of Customs calling an examination or turnout on the vehicle. In addition all food imports had to be cleared with Port Health. This whole circus was enormously inefficient, as most of the paperwork on the Customs side was for the Government Trade figures and nothing to do with duty. I found it quite depressing watching all the freight hanging about for hours where the vehicle was not turning a wheel and earning money. Someone, somewhere had financed the load, which was often worth six figures, and of course the driver(s), on wages, were being paid to do nothing.

One of Olau's many surprising plus points in the early days was that our customs clearances were generally quicker than our competitor ports which in my view did not say much for the rest. Eliminating this bureaucracy is possibly the best and only good argument I have heard for going into the Common Market.

Ole Lauritzen started Olau Line with a freight only service on the 19th November 1974 with the m.v. **Basto V** an 1,877 ton stern loading freighter on charter. He quickly graduated, on seeing the potential, to purchasing the **Olau East** and **Olau West** which were both bow and stern loaders designed for both freight and passenger traffic.

To operate an efficient ro-ro operation you need ships of this type, as vehicles can drive straight on one end and straight off the other. It is also easier to fill up every corner of the ship and thereby get maximum utilisation of the freight/car deck. The disadvantage of these two particular ships was that the freight deck was just over 4 metres high, which resulted in trailers' top tilts touching the deck head and being damaged on occasions when being loaded by tug masters. These ships had a main freight deck with two mezzanines decks on either side which could be lowered to give a lane of cars on each side on two levels with freight and coaches only in the centre.

Although these ships were nothing special they were ships of their time and Ole broke new ground by making catering on board a ferry something to look forward to, not something to avoid.

The ships and the route were an instant success with the lorry drivers and Ole's policy from day one of looking after our freight drivers was established. In the late 70's other routes, particularly those from Dover gave preference to passenger space at peak times due to a general under capacity on all cross Channel routes. Olau always valued hauliers who travelled once a week 52 weeks a year against say the equivalent space in passenger cars that travelled once a year. The value to the Company in £sd is obvious. In short, freight customers began to learn they could rely on Olau.

Sheerness as a port enjoyed excellent industrial relations for many years, albeit at a price, and many is the time when we found ourselves one of the few ports

still operating during industrial disputes. This was always a good opportunity to show potential new customers our service but priority was still always given to existing business.

It was not unusual to have 20 - 40 freight vehicles wait listed on night sailings, but somehow with no-shows, go-shows, and customs bouncing out transit documents we managed to keep everyone happy. Business continued to expand and in September 1975 the **Olau East** was sold and replaced by the **Olau Dana** on charter from DFDS Seaways.

The **Olau Dana** whilst being a nice passenger ship was a stern loader only and not really suited to our type of ro-ro operation, having a general lack of public areas and perhaps too many cabins for the times. Ole Lauritzen had received a good offer for the **Olau East** hence the switch.

In March 1976 the **Olau West** was replaced by the **Olau Finn** (ex **Finn Partner**) on charter from Oy Finn Lines and the **Olau Dana** was replaced by the **Olau Kent,** purchased from Viking Line. The **Olau West** was chartered out.

This was an instant improvement to our tonnage, the **Olau Kent** was a stern and bow loader whilst the **Olau Finn** although being a stern loader had a garage deck above the main freight deck. The freight deck was oddly split into high and low freight space for some reason which we later converted completely to high freight space (4.4m). Both these ships notched up our standards a couple of pegs and again the catering excelled.

Stern loading ships very quickly sorted the men from the boys amongst the freight drivers. Accompanied vehicles and road trains had to be turned on the pontoon and backed, sometimes the full length of the ship into a comparatively tight corner. The Port stevedores of course could do this with their eyes shut but nevertheless it was still a time consuming business.

Olau Line was still expanding rapidly and suffering continuing growing pains as a consequence. Our biggest problem at this time was that we were now

A stevedore turns a trailer prior to backing onboard the **Olau Finn**. The bailey bridge is almost level indicating about 1 metre off the top of the tide. Sheerness has a 30 foot tide and the angle of this bridge, could, on occasions cause considerable problems either in car exhaust pipe damage or knocking sumps off coaches, particularly Volvos.

The original ramp at Sheerness was past its sell by date and a constant source of problems which involved the dockers messing around with bits of wood at certain states of the tide to get an even run off the ship. Ship's ramps are varyingly positioned above the water line and the ramp which has limited adjustment was mounted on a pontoon which could be flooded or pumped out to position it. This was necessary when we ran with the **Olau Finn** and the **Olau Kent.** With two new ships on order the Port was persuaded, for once, to spend some of its own money and provide a new ramp which is seen being lowered into position, early in 1981.

Most freighters had lifts to the weather deck which had to be used for all hazardous cargo. In this view a tug master and trailer ascend the lift of the **m.v. Cap Taillat,** a chartered freighter. Weather, meant what it said, out in the weather

running an unbalanced service - the freight decks, and indeed the car deck space was greater on the **Olau Finn** than on the **Olau Kent** although with certain loads, where we could not use the low freight space they could be the same. This was a marketing weakness as 'what goes out comes back' and we were obliging some of our clients to either use sailings they did not want or return via another operator. This in turn affected their volume discounts on their freight rates.

Following the failure of Dunkirk Ramsgate Ferries in September 1980, the **Olau Kent** on charter to Olau Line, from the owners, was arrested in Vlissingen. This

left us without a night sailing but a replacement was quickly found in the form of the Italian ferry, **Espresso Olbia** (known as the **Olau Ravioli**) which served until March 1981 to be replaced by **Olau Hollandia** (I).

This problem of imbalance continued to dog us until May 1982 when the **Olau Britannia** (I) joined the **Olau Hollandia** (I) which had been in service since March 1981. At last we were able to offer our clients a balanced service with two ships that we owned and the effect was staggering, The trade and our competitors considered us mad to put two luxury ships on our route, but they were an instant success and others too were forced to follow suit.

The first **Olau Hollandia** and **Olau Britannia** (14,550 tons) were both bow and stern loaders with the main freight deck being multipurpose. We had 750 lane metres of 4.4 metre high freight space but a hanging

On her first day in revenue service the new **Olau Hollandia** (I) at North East Spit off Margate in March 1981.

The upper freight deck on **Olau Britannia** (2).

If it had wheels we would carry it, our rates were by metre or vehicle type rather than weight.

deck could be lowered in sections on either side to take cars on two levels as required. This gave maximum flexibility. In addition we had a garage deck which held 56 cars above the main freight deck. The ships were oddly enough bigger sailing from Vlissingen to Sheerness as visa versa. This may sound Irish but the ships loaded through the stern in Vlissingen as against bow loading in Sheerness. This meant that the mate could stow the bow tighter from Holland than was possible from the UK.

Traffic continued to grow even with these new jumbo ferries and throughout the 80's we found ourselves in the spot charter market with small freighters to take up surplus traffic. By the late eighties we had a permanent freighter on service the m.v. **Wesertal** and

Olau found itself with an option for two new 35,000 ton ships similar to those delivered to its sister company TT Line in the Baltic. The freighter also allowed us to build up some hazardous traffic, that is traffic that is prohibited from a passenger ferry ie corrosives, inflammables etc.

The option for new ships was exercised and **Olau Hollandia** (2) was delivered in October 1989 with **Olau Britannia** (2) following in May 1990. These new super ferries had double decker freight decks each of which could be divided by hanging decks to alternatively take cars. They were also bigger on east–west sailings than west-east as with the sisters they replaced. The freighter service was maintained to carry our trailer and hazardous traffic and Olau at last had enough

The main freight deck on **Olau Hollandia** (2) and her sister were like a quarter of a mile of the M25 (the four lane part) picked up, and put inside a ship. The freight deck was multipurpose and the hanging deck above could be lowered in sections as required, depending on the mix of the load.

An Olau sponsored trailer in the Sheerness freight park. All unaccompanied trailers are checked for damage on arrival and a damage report given to the delivering driver. The trailer is then checked against this on collection the other side. Trailers have to have their own M.o.T. and generally have a tough life. A trailer shipment from say Birmingham to Rotterdam would involve two traction companies and two sets of stevedores; one operator told me that a trailer sustains some type of damage on every round trip, not necessarily serious, just 'wear and tear'. Serious damage would constitute a claim against us hence the emphasis on proving if it took place whilst in our care.

space for all its traffic.

In the event the growth we had hitherto seen since the service started, suddenly stalled with the start of the Gulf War which triggered the recession. Although Olau managed to hang onto most of its freight, there was generally less around and as always the rates were very keen. The freighter charter was not renewed from September 1992 onwards and Olau cut back to just the two jumbo ferries. Despite the world recession developing almost into a depression across Europe, we at least managed to get paid for what we carried and although companies were going down like flies, we somehow managed to steer clear of bad debts.

From our inception we always endeavoured to give a service that was special and different, but at the same time we also expected to get paid. After the debacle of the early years we embarked on a scorched earth policy of credit control, by always winding up companies that did not pay and going for the directors if we felt the situation justified it. We were however more prepared to do a deal where we could, and we coaxed many companies back from the brink where the odds seemed impossible. One unusual method that came to my attention for extracting cheques from companies (which Olau never used I hasten to add) was to send an old tramp round to a debtor company with a letter of authority and instructions to wait in their reception until he got a cheque. The Smellie Debt Collection Agency.

In the end Olau's best friend was the tachograph or spy in the cab. Hauliers have to keep the wheels of the vehicles turning but drivers also must, by law, have compulsory rest periods. In the 1970's drivers often got their rest waiting to clear customs but from

The front cover of a special Olau Freightline Brochure we produced to promote the two new jumbo ferries.

January 1993 all of that became old hat. On the short sea routes, or Channel Tunnel for that matter a haulier has to balance the cost of an extra driver against crossing the Channel quickly and a driver then hanging about until his tacho permits him to drive again.

Everyone has to sleep and at Olau we provided the ideal scenario. Drivers could eat, rest and travel all at the same time. Not any more sadly.

SURCHARGES

The world into which Olau was born in 1974 was a xenophobic Britain which like a banana republic controlled its economy by means of the dreaded Exchange Control Act. Briefly this act restricted the flow of Sterling out of the UK effectively acting as a tourniquet stifling investment and trade alike. This was a Socialist measure to support the pound's exchange rate; every time a Labour Government got in, investors immediately pulled their sterling out of the UK selling into a harder currency, this hit the exchange rate and exports, hence the tourniquet. The City does not trust Socialists as traditionally they try to control by legislation something that should be left to market forces. A country's currency exchange rate is like a Company's share price, if the Company makes a loss or the City has no confidence in the Directors everyone dumps their shares.

My first introduction to Exchange Control and this iniquitous Act was a call from the Bank of England inviting us up there for maintaining a Sterling bank account abroad which at the time was illegal for UK resident companies. Oddly enough I was looking forward to this as a rare chance to see the inside of the Bank of England citadel but it was not to be, they

Our 1985 Ferry brochure with prices held at 1984 rates.

called us instead to a crummy nondescript government building in New Change, in the City instead.

Much has been written about surcharges, and much of it is misinformed so it would seem appropriate to take time out to clarify what they are and how they arise.

Every country in Europe has its own currency and in an ideal world we would all be using European Currency Units (ECU's). Europe's economies are not sufficiently aligned to permit so called monetary union so instead we have the Exchange Rate Mechanism or ERM. This is a kind of club where members agree to support each others currencies within certain band fluctuations, the narrow band included those countries whose economies where already closely integrated such as Germany, Holland and France whilst the weaker members lived in a wider band along with Sterling before we dropped out completely. As an aside, if companies conspire here in the UK to support each other's share price it is illegal (remember the Guinness affair) and yet in the ERM these are the rules of the club.

It is easier to understand in terms of Olau's tariff structure. We started from a base line where our rates were set in Pounds, Dutch guilders, Deutschmarks and Danish Kroner at the exchange applicable at a fixed point in time. As Sterling progressively weakened over the years the actual equivalent fare in the different countries would vary to an extent that cute Dutch passengers, for example, purchased their tickets in England in later years. Olau's main expenditure was in the hard Deutchmark whilst 65% of its income was in Pounds Sterling. When the Pound dropped out of the ERM in October 1992 we were suddenly faced with generating another £ 4 million of income annually just to stay where we were. This is not a problem peculiar to the ferry business but in our particular circumstances with our particular combination of currency income and expenditure it hit us very hard indeed.

Everyone does their costings and sets their fares for the forthcoming year based on certain assumptions one of which is the exchange rate. If the rate moves outside the limits of the calculation an exceptional loss or indeed profit situation arises. Many operators, including Olau, reserved the right to make currency surcharges to passengers if certain exchange rate limits were broken. The new EC Package Holiday Directive now requires all operators to set out their exchange rate calculations in their booking conditions and in particular clarify when a surcharge will be triggered.

Although we have charged passengers a currency surcharge in the distant past it is very much a negative marketing tool absolutely guaranteed to upset passengers who inevitably feel they are being cheated. In the end the aggravation, cost of collection, and sums involved made the whole exercise futile. Furthermore as Olau was invoicing passengers in four currencies, a weak pound would be supported by a say a strong Deutchmark and the cost of settling German holiday hotels in the UK would be cheaper. Swings and roundabouts.

Sales on board though would take a bashing as everything was priced in three currencies and the smart money would go on paying by the cheapest method until we reprinted our menus etc. This was solved by pricing everything in Guilders only and holding the exchange rates in the tills instead but a rate change was still a major exercise. It was better on the passenger tariff side to guarantee no surcharges instead which was a marketing tool.

Freight currency surcharges though were different. Unfortunately as a throw back from the days of Sealink and Townsend Thoresen domination all sea freight rates to and from the UK have tended to be in £'s Sterling. To gauge the effect of this when Olau started in 1974 the £ bought 6.5 Dutch Guilders. Today it is nearer 2.9, less than half its 1974 value. Accordingly on the several occasions that the £ went into its periodic free fall, Olau introduced a currency surcharge on sea freight to adjust the loss which would then be consolidated into the next freight increase. To Olau with most its freight income in pounds and its major expenditure in Deutchmarks there is no doubt this was justified but of course most of our customers complained anyway.

As a result, after one of these roller coaster rides six years ago we made a conscious decision to start weaning overseas hauliers off Sterling and onto their local currency to try and hedge our bets a bit more. This was successful in Scandinavia and Germany but the smarter Dutch would have none of it.

Curiously currency fluctuation affects every Company in a different way. Had Olau been an English Company with UK crew and Sterling loans on both its ships, we would have made a windfall profit from our Dutch Guilder and Deutschmark passenger income buying more pounds.

The other common type of surcharge is the fuel surcharge. All oil contracts throughout the world are in US Dollars so it follows that any fluctuation between your home currency and the US Dollar affects your business. In Olau's life we have seen almost Dollar parity at one end of the scale and nearly 2 Dollars to the £ at the other. We have therefore found it necessary to make a fuel surcharge in the past, again on freight, rather than passengers as that tends to be where the greater risk exposure is.

As a last word on surcharges It always seemed an anachronism to me that operators are always quick to introduce surcharges but what happens when the rate goes the other way. I have never heard of an operator yet, who, having benefited from a good pound to Dollar exchange rate refunds this windfall to customers.

For the future the E.C. Package holiday directive requires all operators to publish within their conditions the exchange rates used in their calculations. This is a minefield and what goes up also comes down which is why many operators, Olau included, virtually guaranteed no surcharges.

COMPUTERISATION

When Olau finally closed in 1994 we were operating with the best and most up to date computers that money could buy but it was not always like that.

In the Olau Line of 1974 there was not a computer in sight, electric calculators were taking over from the hand cranked variety, and the electric typewriters we did have were large and very heavy. Manual typewriters were the order of the day. All invoices were hand typed in those far off days, together with all passenger tickets which were also written out and priced by hand; the accounting records were maintained on a large Adler semi automatic accounting machine which was the size of a large desk, with a built in seat. In today's world, the Health and Safety people would probably insist on ear muffs, a seat belt and a hard hat to operate it! Certainly everyone in the building knew when it was in use.

All this was very inefficient and labour intensive, and by late 1980 we were in the advanced stages of persuading our Board to buy an IBM 34 computer. One must never forget though that all capital investment must have a pay back, either in cost savings over its lifetime, or improved efficiency or a combination of both.

Case Rietkerk, on his part, pathologically hated computers and the people that promoted them. He felt, with some justification, that this was the start of an increasingly slippery slope into enormous expenditure, of which in the end you lose control, as you are in too deep to get out. On my part I was more

For many years our passenger tickets were all hand written and produced by a Company in Aylesbury. I once asked to visit their plant when our tickets were being produced and saw the complex computerised quality controls they had using the latest technology with computers and strobes. In this view some of the finished reels are awaiting collation. The ticket run was over 300,000 and when the first tickets were delivered the five part set was found to be out of register (not aligned). The whole lot had to be junked and the job run again. This is an example of the computer legend that goes 'this computer can make more mistakes in 10 seconds than 20 people working flat out for three weeks'.

pragmatic about it but never lost sight of the financial arguments. There was a time to say no as well as yes. In the later years we found ourselves resisting more and more the overtures from our Hamburg head office computer department, as to what they thought we needed, and we thought we could afford.

We were very proud of our first bespoke programs, which had an immediate dramatic effect on our sea freight credit control, and over the next few years more and more aspects of our business were put on the system. Computers handle thousands of similar transactions quickly and efficiently, but it is not cost effective to write a program for something that happens once a year. Computers can also make thousands of mistakes for you, equally fast, if you are careless at the specification stage. Careful testing is an absolute must. Finally everyone should remember that you can programme a computer to do anything you want, and, if you wish, also programme it to forget it has done it. The output is the result of a number of logical program statements which may or may not be factually correct. Just because a computer did it does not make it right.

Meanwhile the first **Olau Hollandia** had come into service and boasted computerised tills and stock control as early as 1980. No other UK ferry was this advanced at this time although our sister company TT Line had used this system in the Baltic for a number of years. All the ships' tills were connected to a central computer which at the end of each round trip produced a floppy disk. This was processed ashore in Vlissingen to give stock and financial control information but also handled the re-ordering of stores. ie '1,265 pints of milk today please milkman.'

The tills however were not fully up to the job at this time, mainly due to the fluctuating voltage onboard ship, and the unavailability of adequate surge protectors in the early 80's. The ships' power came from auxiliary generators at 50 cycles, the same as the shore mains, but the voltage however did tend to have spikes, as most of the ships equipment when switched on tends to draw power in hundreds of amps.

Happily these problems were ironed out and in 1983 the shop tills were all changed for a new Nixdorf system with laser bar code readers which considerably streamlined the whole check out process. Laser tills are everywhere today but at Olau in 1983 we were in on the ground floor.

During the mid-eighties, together with our sister company TT Line, we developed a complete passenger booking system with the main processor and data being in held in Hamburg, with which we communicated through leased data lines. The system also produced passenger tickets and check in lists, with cabin allocations. Cabins were always allocated by the computer to a predetermined ship's plan in respect of the various types available, although it was possible to book a specific cabin and handle round trips with the same cabin both ways. A list went to the ship for cabin cleaning purposes and also to identify any driver who had overslept and was blocking the unloading. Sod's law dictated that anyone who overslept was always parked in a key position blocking

Over the years I travelled to Vlissingen many times on computer related projects, occasionally returning via the short sea routes. In this view my programmer is drawing my attention to rubbish on the deck of another operator's ship. Common decency and politeness prevent me from mentioning the operator or ship.

other passengers or freight, it was never the last person on the ship.

With the new Olau ships in 1989 came a new challenge: coded key card cabins. This was a Norwegian system called Vinco and found in many hotels all over the world. What worried me from the start was how a personal computer (PC) ashore could produce a cabin key for a lock it had never met! There were, so the sales bumph said, some 16 million combinations per lock which was mind-blowing. In fact it was quite logical of course. Each lock was initialised to start with, and then the process worked on levels. The first key for say cabin 100 also told the lock the next 8 combinations to expect. As soon as a later key

code was used the previous one was invalidated and so on. The actual combinations were PC generated and the only thing to really ensure was that everyone changed levels at the same time ie the ten PC's in both harbours and the PC's onboard. The keys were generated as required from blanks together with a paper wallet printed with the passengers name and number. There was no number on the key itself for security reasons.

The new ships had state of the art Computers throughout, not only for the passenger catering side but on the engineering and navigation sides as well. Spares manuals were held on PC's and of course satellite telephone and faxes were on board. The actual bridge was like something out of Star Wars, with all navigation controls triplicated, one set in the centre and one on each flying bridge which were fully enclosed. Older ships tend to have exposed bridge wings for berthing and unberthing but it makes sense for ferries which are docking several times a day to have these enclosed. As one Captain wryly pointed out to me, it was not done to keep the Captain in the warm, more that the Company did not want to get its computers wet !

In the 1990's the world was changing again; more and more travel agents were requiring to book directly into our computer system, which was already possible in Germany and Sweden through 'Start' and 'Smart'. The Association of British Travel Agents (ABTA), who I hold in very low esteem, could have helped everyone considerably here by rationalising their membership numbers years ago, so that every member branch had a unique number for computer recognition. Instead,

Captain Peter Rodehache in between sucking his filthy pipe at the centre bridge consol on **Olau Britannia** (2). The bridge area was enormous on these ships with superb all round vision. The building of all Olau ships have been overseen by one of our Captains and a Chief Engineer who had an office in the shipyard. Captain Rodehache supervised the construction of this ship right down to where he wanted his pipe rack.

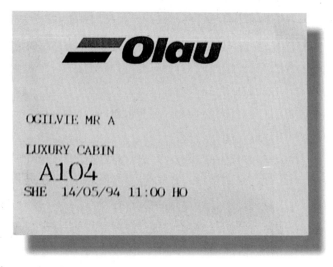

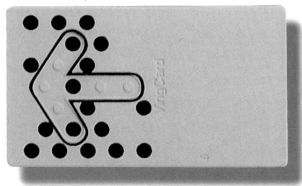

A Vinco key card and wallet.

every travel agent has a different account number with every operator they use. If ABTA had a proper system this could be so much easier for everyone, even their membership numbers have no format or length convention.

For this reason at Olau we ended up with many search 'keys' on our system to correctly identify an agent or customer, we could search on phone number, ABTA number if the agent knew it that is, and many did not, and of course either name or address or town.

In 1990 we got cautiously into bed with American Telephone & Telegraph (AT&T) who were developing a direct booking system for the travel trade. After considerable time, effort, and money a Janet & John version was finally up and running in 1992. A number of other ferry companies subscribed to this system initially to keep their options open whilst actually developing their own software to do this.

At Olau we were not developing our own system but were becoming an increasingly reluctant bride as the costs rapidly escalated. On the user side we found that the marketing of the product by AT&T did not generate the awareness and trade usage we had been led to expect, so the whole thing was rapidly becoming a big expensive white elephant.

In fairness I believe AT&T started in good faith but as costs escalated and users dropped out, either being disillusioned or having developed their own software, there became nothing in it for AT&T. The burden of research and development was falling on fewer subscribers and the initial take up from the trade was disheartening to say the least. Olau finally bailed out as well in 1993 and the whole project seems to have gone very quiet with little or nothing in the trade press.

Another state of the art system which Olau neatly avoided getting involved with was the ATC Automatic Ticket Card. This consisted of a plastic card with a magnetic strip on the back which contained all relevant booking information. Again the cost was enormous but the idea was that passengers just come up to a barrier, put this thing in a slot and drive on the ship. Such a system was pointless for us as there was no

pay back, it would have just been a fancy marketing toy.

By 1994 we only had few remaining areas where further computerisation would have been beneficial such as the production of meal vouchers, boarding passes, and direct debiting of travel agents bank accounts. The latter was a subject very close to my heart as getting our money out of many travel agents was like drawing teeth.

Apart from the above I believe that when we closed we had reached the epitome of computer development for our small two ship operation.

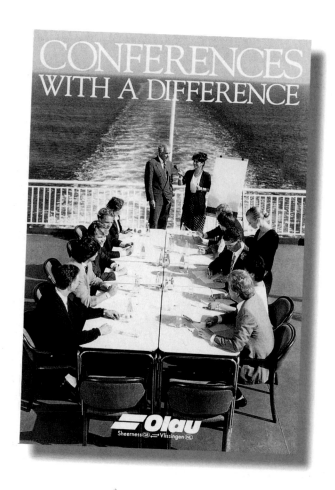

Chapter 5

MARKETING & PUBLICITY

TRAVEL TRADE

For many years now the Travel Agent has been part of the High Street in every town and city throughout the country, but much has changed in the last 20 years.

In 1975 when Olau started the travel agent world was much different to that of today. Apart from the obvious difference, virtually no computers, most were independent, with only small clusters of associated branches, often in or around one area e.g. West London. Thomas Cook was the only real multiple as we know them today.

At that time, as now, there were about 4,500 travel agents who were members of ABTA (Association of British Travel Agents) and about the same number of non ABTA agents. Becoming a member of ABTA involved putting up a bond, employing trained staff and having High Street premises. Membership was supposed to protect the travelling public from the failure of tour operators, airlines, ferry companies etc. The other way to join ABTA was to lie and produce false references. No one however protected Olau from duff ABTA travel agents who well outnumbered failed tour operators. Many agencies tried and failed, some just failed and some were set up to fail.

Olau's first brochure was no more than a tariff leaflet but it did the job.

The non ABTA travel agents which numbered about the same, were referred to as 'bucket shops' in the trade, but from Olau's point of view there was little to choose from the two at the time. We would issue ticket stocks to travel agents if they were members of ABTA, but members came and went so fast that, the ABTA trade directory was obsolete before the print run was finished. ABTA seemed to have no logic to their membership numbers, and re-issued numbers frequently, or used the same number for an affiliated group of shops. An ABTA sticker in an agent's window did not make them members, it means they may be a member, they know someone who is, the previous tenant was etc etc.

In short ABTA lived in a time warp of complacency where nothing was what it seemed to be, but they at least thought they were doing a good job. Notwithstanding this apparent chaotic travel trade situation, Olau's bad debts from the travel trade were generally low, but came from both ABTA agents and bucket shops in equal share. Eventually Olau would endeavour to only give credit to multiples or agents with a good known track record. The ABTA membership in the end meant nothing to us, it was as bad as that.

The 1980's saw a radical revolution in the travel trade as massive polarisation took place, and the all powerful multiples as we know them today emerged as a significant force i.e. Lunn Poly, Pickfords and of course the ubiquitous Thomas Cook. Exchange Travel was also a multiple which caught Olau and many operators and clients alike with their trousers down when they went broke. Nobody seemed to be aware that 50% of the branches were franchise outfits including ABTA who were not sure if they knew or not.

We at Olau spent many thousands of ponds over the years on brochures and their distribution, whilst constantly fielding complaints from agents who claimed to have none.

An internal inquiry always followed which usually culminated in our distributor producing a signed receipt from the complaining agent that brochures had indeed been delivered, and were 'awaiting unpacking' or 'in the basement'. It was often easier for the agent to order more brochures than rummage in their store, it seemed.

Case Rietkerk encouraged all of us, if we were in a strange town to call in at the local travel agent and ask for an Olau Line brochure. The variation of replies we culled from 'trained' counter staff would fill a whole book. My own view was, and still is, that too many travel agents in this country effectively act just as pimps, they get most of the profit and none of the aggravation for a minimum effort.

Many people happily go into a

Everyone has their new brochure printed for the World Travel Market and ready for immediate distribution afterwards. In 1982 this was not to be as a disastrous fire at BP Travel Trade Services destroyed all of Olau's and many other tour operators brochure stock. The reprint took four weeks.

travel agent, any agent, and book an air fare or holiday, and fall into the trap of allowing the agent to relieve them of substantial sums of money, which many just put into deposit accounts before handing it over to the tour operator. Most travel agents do this and are using the principal's money to finance their own business before handing it over less their commission. This situation borders on the criminal since the agent is only entitled to his commission not an interest free loan. It is outrageous that there is no law insisting such moneys are held on escrow, or client account.

As a result the travel world is shifting towards operators direct debiting travel agent's bank accounts when a booking is made. It will be interesting to see how many agents survive when they have to finance their business with their own money for a change.

At Olau we tried not to release travel documents to dodgey agents unless we had the money. On many occasions though we found passengers coming to our terminal expecting travel documents where the agent had failed to mention to their client that the clients' money had not been passed on to Olau.

As a general rule the safest way to pay for anything through a travel agent is by credit card on the tour operators booking form as the credit card company are liable for the value of your trip under the Consumer Credit Act. This is also the safest way for the carrier as the agent then has to make a claim for his commission and cannot get his maws on the tour operator's money.

The 1980's saw a radical change in the travel agent world with many small groups deciding simultaneously they wanted to be big. Initially Olau welcomed this trend as we inherited more outlets and to an extent the credit risk was removed, apart from with Exchange Travel that is.

As if to some predetermined plan, every town in England was losing its identity and becoming a clone of its neighbour. Each had to have a new pedestrian shopping precinct, and within these centres we had the mandatory Boots, Dixons, Granada, W H Smith, Freeman Hardy Willis, BHS, etc., etc., and of course the multiple Travel Agents had to be there as well, in

strength.

In Holland new shops are controlled by the local Chamber of Trade who actually can stop a particular type of shop opening by not granting a licence. If the Chamber feels there are too many, say Building Societies, or the proposed proprietor cannot show competence for a particular type of business then permission is refused. In England no such restrictions apply. Local Councils can and do in certain circumstances refuse planning permission, but the criteria tends to be nuisance rather than unwanted and unnecessary competition or professional competence.

Once the multiples had their toe hold, or rather strangle hold, on the market the tail started to wag the dog. Suddenly racking policy prevailed, and little Olau was effectively blackmailed into paying higher rates of commission, (10% is the industry norm), or 'override' commission to get our brochures racked. Have you ever wondered why some agents had two rows of say Fly-by-Night Tours brochures and a restricted or non existent display for everyone else ? The answer is the best commission rates get the best racking.

In practice at Olau we endeavoured to link over-rides to retrospective turnover but it was a constant struggle and we always felt from then we were racked as a second rate brochure in many multiples.

On my part I felt we should try and take the lid off what we considered a restrictive practice. We could have suggested to ABTA a two tier framework where one type of ABTA membership sticker says something to the effect that this member offers a restricted racking service that pays them the best commission. This line of thought although interesting and perhaps heresy in our business is in fact no different to the way most other retail chains run their businesses.

Dixons for example purchase limited brands, in vast bulk, at the lowest possible price and sell them for the best possible profit margin. This is all the multiple travel agents are now doing; they are no longer 'travel agents' but 'retailers'. I wonder how many of the travelling public realise the subtle difference. What the public now see on offer in a 'retailer' is what is profitable for the retailer to sell, not necessarily the best value to the customer or a comprehensive choice.

Happily there are many good agents but a tendency for high staff turnover in the trade and lack of professional training does find many agents lacking. This is where the multiples score as they are able to run proper courses and train all their staff to a very high level of competence on the particular products they 'push'.

When Olau started about 90% of our business came from the travel trade, by the mid 1980's it was more like 80% and following a deliberate strategy from then we worked harder on direct selling to bring it nearer 70% when we closed. Case Rietkerk did not think as highly of the travel trade as I did, and I did not rate them as a trade very high at all. In fact Case actually mooted on several occasions that we should dump the lot of them and go to direct sell completely, a proposal we seriously considered. Given another couple of years I think we may well have gone this route.

I believe that with the multiples selecting who they

are prepared to rack, this will start an ever increasing trend towards direct selling. The world they have sought to dominate will then collapse around their ears.

As a footnote to this tirade about Travel Agents and ABTA, readers may be re-assured to know that ABTA have just announced new draft rules of membership one of which is that members will no longer be allowed to trade whilst insolvent from the 3lst December 1994, which presumably means its still OK before the 3lst December 1994 ! I am speechless. Now there is nothing anyone can tell me about the travel trade I am not prepared to believe.

BROCHURES

A major part of Olau's tools of trade are brochures and leaflets which were our primary source of communication with our passengers. They also happened to soak up on average about one third of our advertising budget.

Over the years many different agencies have produced our brochures with a varying degree of success. A bad brochure can inexplicably do well if everyone else's is worse, but worse is a subjective judgement and for everyone you ask you get a different answer. It comes down to pushing the right buttons and levers at exactly the right moment and this is an instinct.

In the end the brochure has a job to do: sell the product. The ultimate enigma was always if you have a good year and how do you accurately identify the reason ? External factors also influence sales. For example the year of the Zeebrugge disaster and its far reaching aftermath; in those circumstances the brochure, no matter how good, is eclipsed by

air freight charges.

The real cost in producing a brochure comes in the production and design which is where I was first introduced to 'travel trade English'. It seemed that brochures must be targeted at people with a reading age of six, just like some tabloid newspapers. This revelation came to light after a number of us had punctuated and tidied up the syntax of our proposed brochure one year. We found this sloppiness objectionable but were politely informed by our sales people that everyone else did the same and that was the trade norm.

At Olau we were trying so hard to be different and distance ourselves from the herd so why not produce a brochure in proper English ?

Another exercise I got up to that upset our sales people was to take a brochure to pieces and cost out all the space for holidays against the income generated. This usually gave some surprising results with space occupancy usually bearing little relation to income. Nothing is ever what it seems.

Sales people always have an answer for everything, indeed good sales people could sell sand to the Arabs. In this case the reply was that they were 'stimulating an awareness of the sort of accommodation that is available in Holland'. In short these packages were ringers to make the others look like a bargain, at least I think that is what they were saying ?

When we introduced the new super ferries in 1989 and 1990 we had a major problem. We knew they were the biggest and the best but the opposition had used all the best words before and we had simply run out of superlatives. Even ageing 20 year ships were being described in glowing terms so how could we get our message

Olau Brochures for 1982, 1983, 1984, 1985, 1989.

the ferry industry fighting a rear guard action to neutralise the bad publicity that followed.

Brochure printing has never been cheap but oddly it is cheaper now than it has ever been. This in part is due to new technology but so many companies are hungry now it is a buyer's market. Despite this, quotes still vary by up to 20%. One year (1982 I think) we even printed the brochure in Singapore because at that time it was the best price we could get, and that was after

across?

The answer came in the wrap around brochure where the cover folded out to be quadruple A4. Although this idea had been mooted before, the timing this time was just right and the brochure was a classic and also sold out !

ADVERTISING MEDIA

The Olau Directors had a covenant with our shareholders that only a maximum of 6% of total

The four part 1991 wrap around brochure.

income would/could be spent on advertising and marketing any given year; this figure in turn was arbitrarily split across the four markets of England, Holland, Germany and Denmark of which the UK got the short straw with less expenditure than our proportion of the market. This was, quite rightly, justified on the basis that the fare structure was stronger in Europe so the contribution to the ship was greater.

Many companies have a habit of blowing any balance remaining in their advertising budget at the end of the year because it is there. Indeed I always used to say it's not like real money in sales because that was how it seemed. Any fool can spend money but it is sometimes difficult to balance a sales department's apparent extravagance against encouraging everyone else to put out the lights when they go home. It is still money, and money that has to be earned from somewhere.

It is obviously possible to spend as much or as little as you want on advertising and there are no end of agencies to encourage you to spend. Theoretically

what you spend should be directly proportional to your sales but that assumes effective advertising campaigns, timing and a receptive public.

Our share of the group advertising budget came to around £750-800,000 to include everything and looking back I think this figure was more than adequate. Generally at Olau we avoided National Media advertising campaigns (The Sun, Daily Telegraph etc) as these were extremely expensive and in our view only effective in the 'pile it high sell it cheap' market, the £1 a passenger, which was distinctly where we did not want to be. We did however run small joint campaigns at a National level but as most of our business came from London and the Home Counties, we tended to concentrate on local newspaper advertising.

Our first foray into National advertising had been in February 1977 and was a baptism of fire. At that time we were running the **Olau Kent** and **Olau Finn** which even at that time offered excellent standards compared with our competitors. It was decided to splash out and run a full page colour advert over four

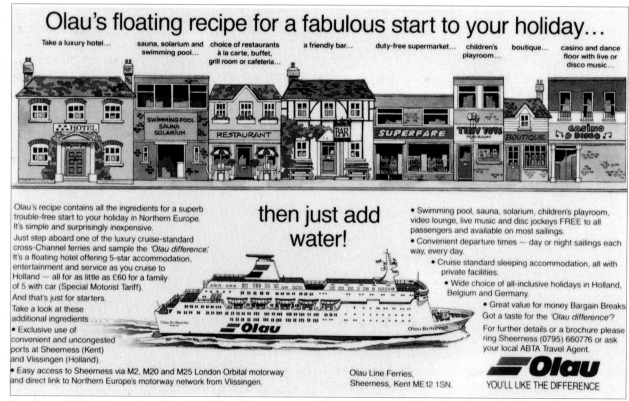

Just ad water . This ad was my personal favourite of all time. It was original whilst being both amusing and eye-catching making a lucid point in a subtle way.

One of our final ads. It says it all.

pages in the Sunday Times colour supplement. The rate at the time was £4000 a page for London and the south east area which blew, as I recall, 10% of our then budget in one go.

Unfortunately the Sunday Times Unions were just starting to flex their muscles at this time, and were in the process of gravely misjudging the proprietors determination to sort them out once and for all.

This was not made clear to us when the advert was placed, with the result that the magazines were printed but not distributed, which was the sort of disruption prevalent at that time. The Sunday Times would not make us a refund, directing us to the force majeure small print, but generously offered, I think it was 15%, discount on our next ad. Some chance !

The key to a good press advertising campaign first is a good advertising agency. At Olau every time we got a new Sales manager they invariably tried to wheel in their own friendly agency, printer, etc., and discredit and kick out the incumbent suppliers on the grounds they could not work with them. This was a common characteristic/weakness of all our sales people and whilst of course it was not the sales manager's decision as to which agency and printers we used, it was important that the two could work together.

Over the years we have used seven different advertising agencies with the last one, which I believe was by far the best, surviving for a record nine years. The important thing is not to let them forget they work for you, and not the other way round. It is their job to be creative and inspirational, and keep you in touch with what the advertising world is doing and any special deals that are around. They must have a good empathy with the product and believe in it but most of all they must not forget that money has to be earned and therefore come up with schemes that are good for the client not just their agency in terms of commission. (see TV advertising).

Not many of our early adverts have survived but this one represents another Olau first. All ferries in the seventies charged for cars by sailing (time of day) and by length. We worked from photostats of Townsend Thoresen's car length tables which we had obtained somehow. This evoked endless arguements with passengers regarding the model of car, did we count the tow bar? What happens if we uncouple the caravan? etc etc. On balance it mattered not a fig as the average was always the same for loading purposes so Olau grasped the nettle and was the first to intoduce a one car length tariff.

Much advertising is placed these days through a media broker, a middle man or as Case Rietkerk calls it putting a hat on a hat. These people take a share but do not add value. Briefly as Olau, or rather our agency, we could not get as good an advertising rate direct from a Publishing House as we could through a media buyer who buys in bulk. Crazy but true. The discount is split, no doubt in their favour, and part of the saving passed on back so everyone wins.

All advertising has to have a message and in our case this was not just a pretty picture of a ship. Olau spent much time and attention on our messages and equal care on where they were placed. A message would be value for money, quality, service, comfort, affordable etc. Generally for every advert that was published another half dozen agency proposals would be rejected and many proposals would not even get beyond working up a rough sketch.

The quickest way to get rid of an advertising budget is to go into television advertising. The advantage of TV advertising as a method of contact with the public is that it is so 'intrusive'; you can pipe your message into the living rooms of everyone watching a given programme in a given area. With newspapers and magazines only groups of readers can be targeted. Television is a catch all and the advantage to the advertising agency is that they make a sack full of money on commission.

Television advertising is sold in bundles by region based on TVR's which means Television Ratings. This is an official yardstick of the number of homes with television in the area you wish to capture. Meridian TV for example, south east region (yes there are two to buy), would cost £30,000 for 200 TVR's. A 200 TVR campaign on all Meridian would cost £75,000 in August 1994 against £120,000 for the same campaign on Carlton and £400,000 for GMTV National.

Olau, with its one route of Sheerness and Vlissingen, was not really large enough to benefit from running a long television campaign although we did run two short bursts over the years. The other ferry operators could share the production costs of making a film (not cheap) together with the enormous air time costs over several routes which gave them a significant advantage.

Television advertising space is sold in packages of slots which are obviously price related. Generally it does not make sense to buy just one slot, say in the middle of the World Cup Final, as it would be inordinately expensive and the television companies would have no ads at other times of the day if everyone did that. A normal small package would give a couple of prime time slots, a couple of soap opera slots with perhaps another six other slots scattered over a couple of days with maybe the odd extra or two thrown in. You can buy as many packages as you want but each region is a separate tariff so you are soon into seven figures, and, a by now, rich advertising agency.

Olau made its first television advert in 1981 to back up the introduction of **Olau Hollandia** (I) which at that time set new standards of Cross Channel excellence, particularly on the catering side. The film was made of a series of stills starting with a bottle of champagne and the cork popping out and following on to views of various ship facilities.

The film was duly made and a number of managers went to a preview showing in London of various versions to make the final choice. In fact the film was the same with slight variations in the soundtrack but I was horrified to see the shot in the sequence of an onboard meal as it was nothing like Olau service. Unbelievably the people that made the film had never been on our ships and the meal in the shot was of battered cod and chips with relish purchased from the greasy spoon restaurant on the corner of Wardour Street. It was then sprayed, with glycerine I think they said, to make it look appetising. As our television slots had been booked, and the agency frightened the daylights out of us with the projected costs of re-mixing the film showing real food, we reluctantly left it as it was.

Olau cuisine, far from the greasy spoon image portrayed in our first Television advertisement.

Every time the ad ran on television I cringed, but nobody else seemed to notice and the campaign was very successful. It's a funny old world.

As a footnote to this, the BBC used the **Olau Hollandia** (I) leaving Sheerness in the videotape at the start of their Holiday Programme later in the year. This was an even greater success as a PR exercise than the television commercial and what is more, did not cost us a bean. There is a moral in this story, I'm not sure what it is, but it's there.

Whilst on the subject of this type of subtle advertising there are other methods of getting on television rather than buying direct advertising space. Many BBC programmes such as Jim'll Fix It for instance use outside locations and being on tight budgets are always on the look out for good television in exchange for tacit free advertising. Needless to say there are middle men who can fix it for you.

Another more crafty method is to pay to have your brand of product, of say cereal in full view on the table in say Coronation Street for perhaps 10 minutes whilst the actors try and remember their lines. This is known as product placement but we never so indulged in this type of advertising as our ships were too big to put on the table in Coronation Street.

Our second television advert was made and run in 1993. We all felt the timing was right for another brief campaign but this time it was on a far more lavish scale involving helicopter shots, actors and musical soundtrack. Once the concept was accepted the first thing was to obtain a licence for the copyright on the music we wanted. This cost four figures for 15 seconds usage, the alternative being to rewrite the whole thing with other music, preferably using someone who was dead and out of copyright. We would still be into paying performing rights though unless we had a rock band on our books.

In reality once the concept is accepted we were virtually stuck with the music irrespective of the price as the two go hand in hand, a fact that has not escaped Equity members. The whole thing is worked up then on a storyboard and then filming starts if all is OK.

The required helicopter shots involved very close up work, virtually under the bows of the ship at speed, to get the effect of the size, power and luxury of the ships. On the day of filming I watched through binoculars as the helicopter buzzed like an angry bee all over the front of the **Olau Hollandia** (2) as she sailed down the Medway Channel. Next day I asked Chief Officer Manfred Boss if it was as dangerous as it looked. "Yes, very", he replied, and after a pause, "but not for us".

The film was duly completed and run in April and May 1993 on South East Meridian backed up by a Trade Press Campaign featuring the star of the film, the Olau teddy.

PUBLIC RELATIONS

The other much misunderstood but essential part of any service industry operation is public relations, (PR). These are people, or a department, whose job it is to convert bad news into good news by manipulating the

presentation, and making any other news good news, i.e. keeping Olau in the public eye in the correct light.

At Olau we made a point of never announcing anything we did not intend to do and never lying to the press. We chose to avoid cheap publicity and do everything we did with dignity. This is in direct contrast with some service companies who have a silly ideas department whose job it is to invent projects for publicity purposes as a way of getting round the back door onto news bulletins. These schemes are usually all fictitious and designed purely and simply to keep their name in the public eye.

In the later years of Olau, when I had more to do with the press, I became increasingly appalled at the way Olau news was written up to be off centre of the truth which had been given out in a press release. There is a saying amongst journalists which goes 'don't let the truth spoil a good story', which means their job is to sell papers not report facts. Much of the Olau missreporting was in my view carelessness in writing up copy but we were very sensitive to damaging inaccurate reports coming very close to issuing libel writs on a number of occasions.

We fluctuated between a PR agency and in house PR over the years with a varying degree of success. The most important thing is contacts and if your PR man or agency does not have good media contacts you are dead in the water and wasting your money.

At Olau we had a cuttings service which culled all references to Olau from any publication in the UK. Unless we had written these ourselves (advertorials) we found that many of these were oblique in their reporting either by giving a misleading impression by leaving out an important relevant fact or just plain misleading. It actually left me wondering just how much of what you read in the newspapers can be relied on.

Remember the maxim, don't let the truth spoil a good story.

TRADE SHOWS

Once a year the travel trade puts on an extravaganza to promote itself called the World Travel Market (WTM). For many years this was held at Olympia but for the last two years it has been at Earls Court the market having outgrown the Olympia complex. It is usually held in November and is the first opportunity everyone has to have a squint at their competitor's fare structures for the forthcoming year.

As a general aside there is in fact a degree of high level contact between ferry operators, but fare structures are strictly taboo. What does happen is a dialogue of discreet red herrings so that everyone was kept guessing until the WTM. At Olau we tended to avoid whatever the word on the street was around and do our own thing based on our own budgets and costings as our fare structure was generally higher than everyone else.

At the WTM virtually all the airlines, ferries, coach operators and large travel agents take stands which in turn are complemented by National stands run by the various tourist boards. The show normally runs for 4 or 5 days with the first two days normally being restricted to trade only.

Another 5 star performance from Olau.

The bear facts:
Date: May 3rd 1993.
Time: 6.30pm.
Programme: James Bond film — Live and Let Die.
TV Channel: Meridian South East.
Subject: The Olau 5 star* experience.
Action: Switch on and **go now**, with Olau.
*For the second year in succession — the only AA five star rated ferry line sailing to Holland.
For further information or reservations ring Sheerness (0795) 666666 or use Ferry# on ISTEL.

Olau
SHEERNESS (KENT) — VLISSINGEN (HOLLAND)
Olau Line (UK) Ltd., Sheerness, Kent ME12 1SN.

The Olau teddy from a trade ad that backed up the television campaign.

A view of Olau's 1993 World Travel Market stand. The organisers tried to encourage exhibitors via their entry rules to bulldoze their stands after each show every year and many exotic stands were so destroyed. We managed, in the end, to design and build a marginally more expensive stand, within their rules, that would have a three year life span so that for year two and three the stand would just be refurbished at a lesser cost. (Olau collection)

At Olau we always felt the WTM to be of dubious benefit as it was very expensive to attend, costing between £20-30,000 each year, was always oppressively hot and generally we felt the money could be better spent. It was however a good opportunity to meet everyone who was anyone in the trade and much business was signed up on the trade days. The question we had to ask ourselves was would that business have come to us anyway had we not been there? That was the ultimate question, the secret of the Universe. Despite serious misgivings we kept going back as a calculated risk as we could not afford not to be there.

The market is arranged around two or three central stages where various National entertainment is sponsored and laid on during the various days. The best pitches are close to one of the stages but newcomers start furthest away from the stages next to the toilets. If Olau re-booked early for the next year, and as people dropped out, our reserved pitch would

shuffle each year inexorably closer to the main hall. On the other hand if we dropped out for a year we were back next to the toilets again. It was a bit like a very expensive game of snakes and ladders and this was our dilemma.

The first task after setting up the stand was to obtain a copy of the opposition's brochures. These would be analysed and their fare structures compared with ours. They of course did the same thing, it was part of the razzamatazz of the show.

Occasionally the odd faux pas slipped through, by way of a printing error but generally at Olau we tried to do our own thing and ignore the suicide pacts on the short sea routes by dumping fares. At Olau we took the view that a travel agent who booked through Olau earned 10% of a reasonable fare but the commission on some of the silly rates on offer through the opposition would often barely cover the cost of the phone call to make the booking.

The other argument is that by fare dumping,

everyone who has booked already on the 'dumped' sailing cancels and re-books at the cheaper rate. It is common sense and all this achieves is diluted income and a lot of administration to boot. Case Rietkerk's view was if we sell fares for a £l, which incidentally just covers port taxes, how can £20 plus fares be justified? People would feel we were cheating them.

Of course, as with all travel trade do's much wining and dining went on and in fact in the 1970's most tour operators had a resident inebriate on their books specifically for this purpose. Never before since time began has an industry spent so much money entertaining themselves. The essential pre-requisites it seemed for attending the WTM were a lot of stamina and a strong liver.

Olau attended many other trade shows around the country and of course the County Shows and £ for £ these were generally much better value. County fairs were more of a lottery though as being in the open they were either a fantastic success or an absolute washout. The weather seemed to hate county shows as summer heat waves are frequently briefly punctuated by vicious gales of wind and torrential rain, usually during show week. Certainly it puts hairs on your chest working a County Show and I don't just mean the men.

Once a year ABTA holds a conference of its membership to which many tour operators and carriers attend and sponsor 'events', to promote their particular products. These are on a somewhat grander scale than for example the TUC conference which traditionally meets in the industrial heartland of England.

ABTA on the other hand really go for it when they have a conference with such venues as Acapulco, Buffalo, Australia, Palma etc., after all why not? 'conferences' are tax deductible and holding one in say Halifax would not have the same ring about it. Perhaps one day it will even be held on the moon, providing there is a 24 hour fully licensed bar there of course.

Olau's demise will at least release our pitch at the World Travel Market this year and some lucky exhibitor can shuffle their stand one step nearer the centre stage. The show must go on.

SPONSORSHIP

Virtually everyone who gets media exposure these days is involved with sponsorship either blatantly with sponsor badges or subtly with say their brand of cereal on the table in Coronation Street. The game's the same, using the media to create awareness of your product and promote your brand or logo.

At Olau we were always dubious about the benefit of such advertising mainly because the whole thing is so expensive to do properly and we were not in that league. Our advertising budget, under a covenant with our shareholders, was only 6% of our total revenue. In the UK by the time we got our share we were looking at between £750,000 - £800,000 which would not even buy one formula one racing car engine for example. Out of our budget we had to print and distribute our brochures, about £200,000, have a presence at the trade shows, £75,000, run a media campaign

The author tries out for size a the racing car of Kees van der Gent sponsored by our Dutch office in 1976.

£400,000 and what was left was for expenses, give-aways, and sponsorship.

Given these restrictions what we did do was very limited and relatively low key. Careful thought went into what we did and the potential media coverage. Sponsoring racing cars or bikes for instance would earn us an OLAU flash on the side of the machinery but who can read it at 100 mph plus and of those that can, does OLAU mean anything ? For this reason in the UK we tended to confine motor racing sponsorship to free transport of the racing team in exchange for a sticker. The alternative would be to paint the whole thing in our colours in exchange for the whole bill, all the space is for sale after all.

At Olau we were marketing a luxury product, a restful way to travel where time seems to stand still and for this reason one of the methods we did adopt was sponsoring a balloon envelope. This thing went all over the country with its support vehicles and was seen by many thousands of people. It seemed to us to epitomise the dignified sedate type of travel we offered.

Apart from being famous for cheese and windmills the Dutch have also made flowers very much their business and Olau brought millions of exotic blooms to the UK over the years. In England probably the most famous flower festival is the one held at Spalding every year, which apart from being a major media

Case Rietkerk and Johan van Boven of Olau Line, Vlissingen chat with Noel Edmonds at the Truckfest.

The Olau float at the Spalding flower festival of 1993.

event was right in the opposition, Stena Sealink's, back yard. Olau sponsored this event for three consecutive years and entered a float every year thereafter until we closed .

Any return on sponsorship, of course, is very difficult to quantify although the advertising agencies claim to have various scientific ways of measuring this based mainly on statistical sampling. I was deeply mistrustful of such exercises and felt we had struck the right balance, a very cautious involvement in such ventures.

Perhaps our most extravagant sponsorship was of the Truckfest. This event is held annually at Peterborough and is a family day out based around large goods vehicles of all descriptions.

Over the years we received numerous requests for prizes for raffles etc., and generally these were granted on the general proviso that the organisation was non profit making. It was often flattering to see the prize priority list particularly if another ferry operator had also given a ticket as this subtly confirmed our state of esteem or otherwise in the organiser's eyes.

Our last sponsorship flings were sponsoring the Kent County Youth Cricket Team in 1993 and the Round Rochester Cycle Race.

Sales departments are always full of hot air and ours was no exception. In this view some of it is put to good use in the Olau balloon.

Chapter 6
PHOTO INTERLUDE

Although this book is profusely illustrated it contains but a fraction of the pictures I have taken over the years. This photographic interlude is a personal selection of pot pourri with hopefully something for everyone.

The **Olau Finn** leaving Sheerness in June 1976.

The **Olau East** on our berth in the inner harbour Vlissingen in March 1976 (Olau Collection)

The **Olau Finn** arrives in Sheerness for a trial berthing in March 1976. We were initially horrified at her size and opulence for a passenger ferry but she was an instant success and served us well over the next 7 years.

Apart from the Olau route, Sheerness' other claim to fame was the wreck of the **Richard Montgomery**, a wartime Liberty Ship wreck still loaded with explosives. This is a silly season story that regularly gets re-cycled during the summer in one of the National papers that is short of news. The ship foundered on the Sheerness Middle Sand on the 20th August 1944 and broke in two, now, three pieces. It is regularly surveyed and does still have some shells and explosives in its hold which the experts deem best left there. This view is from the ferry which used to pass the wreck about 50 metres distant. For some time, although not so much recently, munitions were washed ashore on the Sheerness beach usually after a northerly storm. Most people called the bomb disposal squad but for a while, incredibly, we had a spate of people walking these things through the town and handing them in at the police station! Needless to say the police were not amused. The Liberty ships were of all welded construction and built on a production line basis, L A Sawer in his definitive book on Liberty Ships reports that in a special effort for publicity purposes one of these ships was launched after ten days and delivered five days later, barely long enough for paint to dry properly. The previous record for complete manufacture had been forty seven days.

At sea on the **Olau Finn,** the flags are the Olau house flag, the Finnish national flag, as the **Olau Finn** was registered in Helsinki, the white and red H flag- 'I have a pilot on board', and the Dutch courtesy flag for entering Dutch waters. Finn Lines are actually a management company for people who own one or more ships but want to operate them under the Finn Lines banner. The actual owner of the **Olau Finn** at the time was a greengrocer!

The **Olau Finn** arrives and turns in Vlissingen. This view shows clearly the new Vlissingen link span and the passenger walkway which ran alongside it.

A rare and unusual visitor to Sheerness in April 1978 was the P&O Jet Foil **Flying Princess.** En Route from London to Zeebrugge she had hit something in the water damaging her sufficiently to have all the passengers put off in Sheerness and re-routed via Dover.

As Townsend Thoresen introduced their new super ferries they each did a Blue Riband run from Dover to Calais. A number of Olau Managers, myself included, booked on the crossing on the **Spirit of Free Enterprise** to check out the new service and be part of history. As I drove on they gave me a free ticket for another trip and offered to take our picture and send it to our local paper, an offer which we tactfully declined. The atmosphere on board was incredible and when the Captain put power on the water at the stern boiled and spewed up over the link span. We shot out of Dover harbour and crossed in quite a rough sea, pierhead to pierhead, in 52 minutes 52 seconds, exactly 1 hour from berth to berth. It is now deemed safe to release the above snap for publication where the now unemployed author is endorsing another ferry product.

A splendid view of the **Olau Finn** in the Medway Channel taken from the Crescent Shipping Thames Barge **Cabby** (Bill Moses).

The **Espresso Olbia** (Olau Ravioli) arrives at Sheerness for the first time in October 1980.

The **Olau Finn** leaving Sheerness as viewed from Port Operations at Garrison Point.

Sheerness is also one of the country's busiest lifeboat stations maintaining a full time Waveney class boat the **Helen Turnbull** and an inshore lifeboat (ILB). The launches in the early Olau days were two maroons for the ILB and three for the main lifeboat, whose Coxwain, Charlie Bowry worked for Olau. When a storm blew up he would encamp in my office smoking his rotten pipe waiting for the inevitable shout. Although the port had a kind of gallows at Garrison Point where the dreaded black storm warning cones were hung there usually was someone who was caught out. A northerly hooligan often drove the maroons down onto the roof of our office before they exploded. This was always exciting and at least it kept us all regular. In this view the **Helen Turnbull** is trying to outrun the **Olau Finn** out of Sheerness. Launches are dull affairs these days as high tech has taken over and all the lifeboat crew have bleepers.

An aerial view of the **Olau Finn** in 1980 sporting her scheme applicable to the Ole Lauritzen/German Partnership.

The **Olau Kent** in her final livery sails up the Thames estuary towards Sheerness in the summer of 1980.

Before settling on building new ships we cast around for suitable existing ships for many months. This **Olau Hollandia** is the ship that never was. She was the m.v. **Cabo San Sebastian** which together with her sister the m.v. **Cabo San Jorge** would have been our new fleet. We looked at these ships very hard, even to the extent of producing these publicity mock ups, but all fell through at the last minute partly due to the asking price and the owners wishing Olau retain the Spanish crew.

The Carvery Restaurant - **Olau Hollandia (2)** (Ferry Publications Library)

The Las Vegas Bar **Olau Hollandia (2)** (Ferry Publications Library).

The first Olau berth in Sheerness from **Olau Hollandia** (I). The new ships were larger than anything we had used to date and berthed bow on to this pontoon with the bulbous bow ending up just short of the front of the pontoon. At the time we had no emergency berth so took out 'foul berth insurance' against the risk of putting ourselves out of business. The round dolphin on the corner is a revolving doughnut for the ship to lean on at certain states of the wind and tide.

Olau gave a gala dinner in Sheerness in March 1981 to promote the new **Olau Hollandia.** The guest of honour was Lord Astor of Hever seen here being formally announced by the toastmaster.

A Royal Marines Band and the opening of the bow of the **Olau Britannia** (I) for guests to board just after the Christening.

Christening a ship is always a moment of extreme tension followed by elation, providing the bottle breaks that is. At Olau steps were taken to make sure the bottle broke, and in this view the joy and relief are clear on the faces of Captain Bohn, Master of the **Olau Britannia** (I), HRH Princess Margaret, Countess of Snowdon and Heinz Kerstan Managing Director of Olau Line. The bottle of champagne is held in a cradle over the bow which is released by the ships' telegraph in the foreground.

The **Olau Hollandia** (I) leaving Sheerness in March 1991 on her first revenue earning service.

This superb model of the **Olau Britannia** (1) was made by the Thanet Catering College from icing sugar and presented to the ship on the 7th May 1982. It was placed in the restaurant next to the Captain's Buffet but after a few weeks we noticed smaller passengers were apparently eating the lifeboats! Accordingly the model ship was 'drydocked' in the ship's kitchen for repairs and incarcerated in a glass case by our carpenters to keep little fingers off in the future.

The view from the bridge of **Olau Britannia** (1) of the m.v. **Wesertal** on our second berth in Vlissingen.

The view from the bridge of the **Olau Hollandia** (1) having just left Sheerness. The fin on the top of the funnel created a draught of fast moving air below to lift and carry smuts clear of the stern.

Both the new ships experienced minor problems over the years from time to time with their bow visors usually as a result of being hit by large waves. In this view the **Olau Hollandia** (1) is seen stern on in Sheerness whilst work proceeds inside to free the offending hydraulic bolts.

Perhaps the most famous model village in Holland is at Maduradam just outside the Hague. In 1985 Olau sponsored a model of the **Olau Hollandia** (1) and the above view is the official hand-over ceremony. Maduradam is a charitable trust set up by a Dutch family who were well heeled but lost both their sons in the war. There were so saddened by the terrible loss of life, particularly young lives that they founded Maduradam for the perpetual enjoyment of children. They say the only difference between men and boys is the size of their toys and so it is with Maduradam, it is really for all the family.

During 1988 P&O European Ferries had a full strike on all their ships which were tucked away in Holland to avoid them being occupied. Some were sent to Rotterdam but three were mothballed in what we called the P&O Garden of Rest and Remembrance in Vlissingen's inner harbour.

The **Pride of Portsmouth** formerly **Olau Britannia** (2) pictured leaving Portsmouth on 6th August 1994. (Miles Cowsill)

Color Lines **Christian IV** formerly **Olau Britannia** (I) at Kristiandsand. (Philippe Holthof)

A unique view of the Olau twins together at Vlissingen with the **Olau Hollandia** (2) on the left and the **Olau Britannia** (2) on the right. (Alan Ogilvie)

The New **Olau Hollandia** and **Olau Britannia** at Sheerness. (Fotoflite)

FREIGHTERS

Olau's policy was always to try and match its tonnage to its demand and this necessitated chartering many freighters for varying periods over the years in fact in a couple of cases for as little as one day.

m.v. **Belinda** viewed from **Olau Hollandia** (2)

m.v. **Imola.** This ship was chartered for a short time to carry Vauxhall Cars displaced during the summer season by passenger traffic. It is actually being pulled in by a tug on its first day which was a good start.

m.v. **Autoroute** viewed from Port Operations, Garrison Point.

m.v. **Jarama** another small car carrier for a small spot charter.

m.v. **Nordborg** viewed from Sheerness No 1 berth

m.v. **Argo** passing **Olau Hollandia** (1) in the Medway Channel.

m.v. **Naesborg** passing **Olau Hollandia** (1) in the Medway Channel.

m.v. **Stena Topper** on the new Olau berth at Sheerness from the **Medway Surveyor.**

m.v. **Kaprifol** at Vlissingen on our second berth.

m.v. **Ramsgate** approaching Sheerness from Garrison Fort.

m.v. **Wesertal.**

The **Olau Hollandia** (2) pictured off the Belgium Coast. P&O European Ferries freight vessel **European Seaway** can be seen on passage from Dover to Zeebrugge. (Fotoflite)

The **Olau Britannia** (2) approaches the Sheerness linkspan on her maiden voyage on 21st May 1990. (John Hendy)

m.v. **Mercandian Supplier II** passing the West Cant Buoy just off Garrison Point.

THE GREAT STORM 16TH OCTOBER 1987

It is said that everyone remembers where they were when President Kennedy was assassinated. Although most people in the South of England were in bed on the night of 15th and 16th October 1987, nobody will ever forget that storm.

On the morning after the storm the inbound **Olau Hollandia** (I) was not on the berth at 7.00 a.m. which was no surprise and a call from Captain Mantei at 8.30 a.m. confirmed that he had anchored off Margate to ride out the storm, but was now on his way.

The damage in the docks was substantial, apart from trees being blown down, buildings had suffered severe damage, trailers had blown over, 300 of the 1200 Vauxhall cars for which we were responsible had varying degrees of damage but worst of all 3 enormous 150ft dock cranes had been blown off the No I berth into our berth.

In addition, all the Port's service vessels had foundered at their moorings briefly making them a land based operation and our berthing pontoon was flooded out and damaged, again.

The **Olau Hollandia** (I) was held at the Medway Buoy whilst we waited for the weather to subside enough for the Port to send down a diver to locate the cranes.

With a 30 foot tide there was a very real chance that the ship could settle on one of these obstructions.

Having received the 'all clear' from the Harbour Master the **Olau Hollandia** (I) berthed just after 1.00 p.m., 6 hours late. Captain Mantei who had sailed the world told us it was the worst sea he had ever seen anywhere and whilst the ship was never in any danger he had taken shelter off Margate and anchored, head to wind, to ride out the storm. This was for the comfort of the passengers and to minimise the chance of damage to the bow visor and equipment on board.

Captain Mantei also had another tale to tell. At the height of the storm his ship had been pushed

The **Olau Hollandia (I)** berthed on the day of Great Storm. Storms of Biblical proportions were often followed by brilliant sunshine and a weird stillness such as this. It was almost as if nature had contrived to show the best and worst it could do just to remind everyone who was the boss.

backwards, the anchor brake had caught fire and 180 metres of chain had run out tearing the retaining shackle from the port anchor locker. We were given the exact position of the lost anchor and chain with a view to our hiring a salvage boat to retrieve it as soon as possible. This had not been mentioned in any of the calls via the VHF to and from the ship as there are always people listening somewhere to make some money. The ship was reloaded and sailed at 3.00 p.m. on the 16th October, four hours late.

Like a huge dead insect, one of the dockyard cranes lays along the Ports No 2 berth.

The **Olau Hollandia** (I) sailed at 3.00 p.m., 4 hours late whilst in the foreground the **Medway Rhino**, having been pumped out itself prepares to start the crane salvage operation.

The first crane is recovered from the harbour three days later. (Olau collection)

In this view a tanker trailer, whilst being unloaded from **Olau Hollandia** (I) lays on its side having slipped off a tug master and landed half on and half off the ramp. Miraculously nobody was hurt.

The **Olau Britannia** (I) had fared better by running before the storm, in that almost, most of the weather was behind them. Captain Heilmann also reported it was the worst sea he had ever seen. On board they had kept the barograph trace to show us which registered 955 millibars, which was almost off the bottom of the paper and the lowest any officer on board had ever seen. Both ships suffered minor damage to crockery and glass but no passengers were hurt and there was no cargo damage.

As a foot note when the salvers we had engaged arrived off Reculver to recover our anchor and chain they could not find it. This was a complete mystery as the Captain had noted the exact position and said nothing on the VHF. We too had kept the lid on it ashore.

Two weeks later our freight manager in Vlissingen received a call from someone who started 'I hear you may have lost an anchor........'. With anything to with ships it is amazing how there is always someone ready to do a deal, and so it was, within days we had bought our own anchor and chain back and it was firmly back in place on the port forecastle.

Perhaps a fisherman found it with his sonar and made a phone call, who knows? We never did find out.

Although the tank was on its side and fouling the ramp it did not impede the discharge or indeed re-loading of the ship.

ANATOMY OF A MISHAP

Any place where heavy equipment is in use is potentially dangerous and docks are no exception. Accidents were rare at Olau and usually when they did occur tended involving something sticky. The following sequence is of a spectacular accident that occurred whilst unloading **Olau Hollandia** (I) in April 1983.

Loading continues past the stricken tank trailer which by now is leaking, guess what - glucose!

By the time loading is complete a heavy lifting crane brought in by the port is set up to right the tank trailer.

The lift commences. Note the extending legs to stabilise the crane and give it a broader centre of gravity.

This rear view of tug master No 5 after the accident clearly shows the hydraulic pistons that lift up a trailer from its dolly legs prior to moving it. The flat plate on the top has a king pin which should lock and couple the tug to the trailer. The tugs fuel tank has been knocked off by the tank as it went over. Number 5 was a rogue tug master as if a trailer did fall off it was always number 5 that was involved.

The tank is semi righted and checked to allow the **Olau Hollandia** (I) to slip back on her berth and depart.

A cautionary tale for the careless. Pictured in Vlissingen harbour a few months after this incident a similar crane that was unloading tree trunks from a barge. The driver, who survived, had apparently not done physics at school.

SECOND GENERATION SHIPS

With new ships on order a new berth had to be provided at Sheerness. This involved reclaiming 10 acres of land to the North East of Garrison Point Fort, in this view work has just commenced.

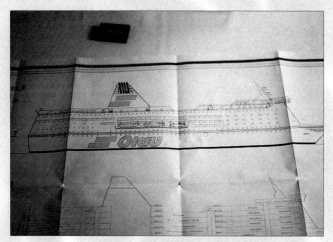

Another Olau ship that never was. Before taking up the option to build the new **Olau Hollandia** and **Olau Britannia** at Seebeckwerft a number of other proposals were considered including this one from a Taiwanese shipyard.

In order to get our passengers from the terminal to the ships, the Garrison Point Fort was used as a satellite. In this view the walkway connection is being made through one of the casemates.

In this view the walkway from the ship passes through the battery arches. The stone in the left foreground has been chamfered off at the base to allow the long removed guns to swing. The large hooks on the ceiling were for moving the guns whilst the small hooks were for the hammocks of the gun crews. The casemates were made into windows, all but one, which was preserved as was. These vaulted arches had been plugged with concrete during the war and this all had to be removed.

The near completed passenger walkway from the fort to the ship.

The new Sheerness linkspan being lowered into position in the summer of 1989. (Olau collection)

A water display from one of the Hamburg fire tugs as **Olau Hollandia** (2) eases up the Elbe to St Pauli pier, in Hamburg on her maiden voyage.

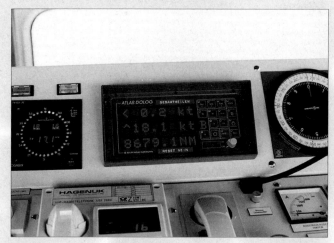

The 'speedometer' on **Olau Britannia** (2). This is the Atlas Dolog which shows the true speed over the ground and true tidal drift. In this view the ship is making 18.1 knots forward with a 0.2 knot current from the starboard side. The instrument on the left shows the wind is coming from North, North East at a speed of 17.1 metres per second.

MISCELLANEOUS

Olau Hollandia (2) arriving at Sheerness for the first time in October 1989

We carried many unusual loads over the years; in this case a steam launch manufactured by Ernie Spears of Bay Class Yachts for a German customer, Herr Wilhelm von Fink. I was lucky enough to have a run in this during the beating of the bounds ceremony and was surprised by its silent running, incredible acceleration and complete lack of vibration. The engine was a two cylinder 15 horse power compound running on coal (remember that black stuff Arthur Scargill wanted us all to use).

The Royal Artillery Band play the German National Anthem as Olau Britannia (2) arrives at Sheerness for the first time in May 1990.

The presentations that follow a successful Christening, in this case of Olau Britannia (2) Lucinda Green shares the moment with 7 year old Verity Ellinor, with Captain Rodehache, Captain Heilmann and Olau Chief Executive Martin Bellmann looking on.

Captain Mantei's view from the bridge of Olau Hollandia (2). Having turned his ship in Vlissingen harbour he is backing down to the Olau freight berth next to the new Olau Britannia (2) on the 20th May 1990.

Olau Line was not required to carry a Doctor providing a number of ships officers held advanced first aid certificates. In mid Channel we were three and a half hours from either port and a helicopter could be organised within twenty minutes in an extreme emergency. The English and Belgian Airforces regularly practised dropping a man on board and picking him up again. In this view a Belgian helicopter has landed a man and is circling the ship prior to recovering him after he has visited the Duty Free shop.

Two jumbos for a jumbo ferry. Part of Jerry Cottel's Circus these two big customers have just had their passports checked by Customs. We had organised a press photocall but Customs pulled one of their annoying stunts by insisting they inspect all the health certificates and animal passports for the whole circus, which believe me was a circus. The animals were of course exercised and fed en route although these two particular customers were not allowed to eat in the restaurant.

The stacking lanes in Vlissingen. Once passengers had checked in and cleared immigration they are held here for loading instructions.

The illuminated ships name of **Olau Britannia** (2) located behind the bridge. The **Olau Hollandia** nameplate was white letters on blue. Ships are traditionally named after women and in any case always referred to in the feminine gender. This is reputably because ships, like women, are difficult to handle.

During his 1991 election campaign John Major visited Sheerness and changed his fortunes by standing on his now immortal soap box. He is seen here checking out Olau for floating voters. (Olau collection)

For a while one of the rougher pubs in Sheerness was the Britannia which finally closed in August 1992. It was acquired by David Sevier, our company solicitor who converted it into offices for his firms use with a planning covenant to retain the old pub facade, including the sign. It therefore seemed a good idea to restore and update the old Charrington sign reflecting the premises new use and depicting the **Olau Britannia** (2). Left to right David and Mariejeanne Sevier, and George Button, the artist. (Olau collection)

The Thames estuary is littered with the remains of wartime defences. In this view are the Maunsell Towers on the Shivering Sands off Herne Bay viewed from **Olau Hollandia** (2). During the war they each had anti aircraft batteries on the top and in the sixties became pirate radio stations. They were for many years connected by catwalks but these were cut away by the Ministry of Defence in the 1980's to discourage further trespassers.

For the publicity launch of **Olau Hollandia** (1) we produced a limited edition beer in conjunction with Kent brewers Shepherd Neame. These were very limited and put out on the tables for the gala luncheon so very few survived, mine only did because I seemed to be running errands all through dinner and barely had a chance to sit down. These now change hands in Exchange & Mart for around £40. Somehow the **Olau Britannia** (1) missed out on having its own brew but for the two new ships we did it again only this time giving a bottle to everyone who shared in our special day.

A regular traveller on Olau was Geoff Capes who is seen here picking up a couple of Olau staff. Geoff was a kind gentle giant who was once travelling back to Sheerness on the **Olau Hollandia** (1). In the early morning there was a disturbance in one of the cabin corridors but outside guess who's cabin. The two people involved disturbed Geoff who asked them to be quiet; they chose to ignore this very sound advice and decided to take him on instead. This proved to be a big error of judgement.

Olau Hollandia (1) leaving Sheerness for the last time in October 1989 escorted by the ubiquitous Knight's Navy to become the m.v. **Nord Gotlandia.** Although Knight's did not earn much money from Olau, as our ships were designed not to need tugs, they always showed us every courtesy and kindness. They were completely honourable people who it was a pleasure to work with and we never had any arguments with them on the basis of any charges. This is in contrast to taking a tug in Vlissingen which was a minefield for the unwary, as there were quite a few cowboys around. They say it took God six days to build the world and on the seventh the Dutch built Holland. Whether that was true or not the Dutch certainly make the sea, controlling it, and earning money from it, their business.

A superb night shot of **Olau Britannia** (1) on our old berth in Sheerness. (Olau collection)

Chapter 7

THE FERRY WORLD

MONT LOUIS

On the 25th August 1984 off Ostende the Westbound **Olau Britannia** (I) en route to Sheerness collided with the CGM freighter m.v. **Mont Louis** en route from Dunkirk to Russia. The m.v **Mont Louis** had stopped to drop its pilot, and in poor visibility, drifted across the fairway into the path of the **Olau Britannia** (I).

The ships were locked together for some hours whilst each was surveyed internally to ascertain if both ships would float and/or who was holding who up. After some 4 hours two tugs pulled the stricken **Mont Louis** free of the **Olau Britannia** (I) and towards a

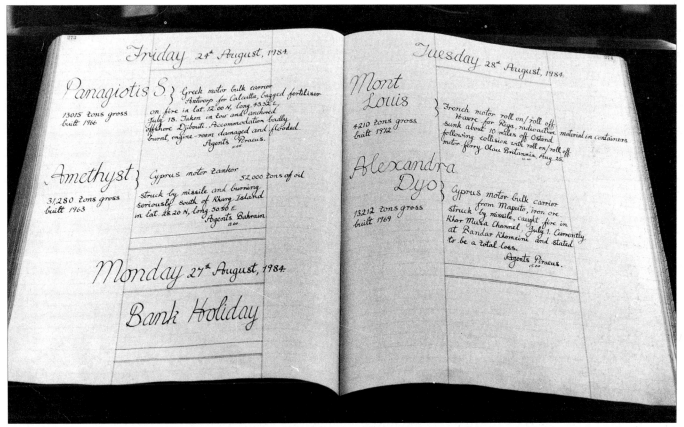

The Loss Book at Lloyd's of London and the entry of 25th August 1984. Large losses used to qualify for ringing of the Lutine Bell but this is kept now for ceremonial occasions only. (Lloyd's of London)

An aerial view of the ships locked together as printed in a Dutch newspaper the following day.

The m.v. **Mont Louis** sinking. (Olau collection)

A lorry that has run forward in the ship on its brakes and collided with the forward hanging deck.

visor on the pontoon.

Initially the inside car deck of the **Olau Britannia** (I) resembled a multiple crash on the motorway but closer examination revealed only minor damage to a few passenger cars. A freight lorry had sustained the most serious damage, probably due to faulty brake application whilst two trailers had also slipped off their trestles and damaged a coach. We had been faxed the loading list from Vlissingen and already knew the positions of the damaged vehicles on board; these were quickly cleared by the stevedores who were on hand with all the necessary jacks and fork lifts etc. The Sheerness stevedores may have been expensive but if ever we had operational difficulties they were quick and efficient at sorting it out.

The ship was cleared and reloaded, all vehicles having to be backed on as the bow was effectively

The **Olau Britannia** (I) arrives at Sheerness the day after the accident looking distinctly battered.

shallow sand bank where she capsized and sank.

The **Olau Britannia** (I) was deemed safe to continue to Sheerness where she arrived at 22.00hrs. We had to take her stern on in Sheerness as the bow visor, which now resembled a shark's mouth, was badly damaged. In fact the bow visor is cosmetic and was the source over the years of many ill informed experts writing to the press saying we were in the habit of sailing with our bow doors open. The truth is that the main car deck in the bow has a watertight collision bulkhead, which is further protected by the loading ramp, which was also watertight. The bow visor, which was cosmetic, then closes on the front. The bow visor would only close when the ramp was raised and at Sheerness at least was actually closed during the ships first manoeuvre backing from the berth. The reason for this was to avoid catching the base of the

The **Olau Britannia** (I) in dry-dock in Bremerhaven showing the temporary bow repair and prior to having the whole bow section amputated. (Olau collection)

sealed due to the damaged visor and associated hydraulics. Meanwhile the surveyor for the hull underwriters went about his work and quickly declared the ship seaworthy giving clearance to sail, which she duly did just before midnight, two and a half hours late.

The bow visor was strengthened and made good in Vlissingen and we were back in business, or so we thought. The next day however some papers ran a story that the m.v. **Mont Louis** was carrying nuclear material which caused a major panic amongst many of our passengers who had been on board. Nevertheless Olau had the ship surveyed for radioactivity the next day in Sheerness and in fact my wrist watch read higher than the **Olau Britannia** (I) on the Geiger counter.

Despite this many passengers were more than a little upset, the m.v. **Mont Louis** was now 'downstairs' and as yet it was too early for a salvage team to have surveyed the wreck. Meanwhile CGM, the French owners were being deliberately evasive about what exactly was on board which merely fanned the flames. It did however take the pressure off Olau as everyone knows the French are not adverse to selling anything to anyone providing it was made in France. All we could do was confirm that our survey for radioactivity was negative but suggest people go to their local hospital for a check up if they were still worried.

We were now back to a stern loader only, just like the old days with the **Olau Finn.** The next job was to seek quotations to repair the **Olau Britannia** (I) and we

made another discovery. Although we had detailed drawings of the ship they were not it seemed sufficiently detailed enough for another yard, other than the yard that built the ship, to fabricate a new bow without having the ship on hand. The demurrage of taking the ship out of service whilst a new bow was manufactured to fit was out of the question, so the ship went back to Seebeckwerft in Bremerhaven for the repair.

Impressively the actual repair was done virtually overnight in a floating dry dock. Basically the damaged area was amputated back as far as the last undamaged plate and a new bow, one they had made earlier, welded into place. The whole operation was very slick and when this was done you could only see the join if you knew exactly where what to look for it. The new bow included a new visor, ramp and collision bulkhead with all the ancillary electric and hydraulics connections to make it work.

As a footnote, many months after this incident we received in Sheerness a writ from King Baudouin, King of the Belgians representing the Belgian Government. This was for the removal of the wreck of the m.v. **Mont Louis** off Ostende. This document was stunning with beautiful scrollwork, a work of art in fact, forgetting for one moment that it actually represented potential litigation against Olau. It was forwarded post haste to our head office in Hamburg, unfortunately without my taking a copy.

I later enquired as to the outcome and was told the

A view of the bow of **Olau Britannia** (I) following the amputation of the damaged section which included the visor and ramp leaving the collision bulkhead intact.

A full car deck on **Olau Hollandia** (2). Note the two orange arrows on the centre bulkhead below the clock. These are the ships built in stability indicators.

case had been thrown out of court as the writ was not against the owners of the **Olau Britannia** (I) but Olau Line (UK) Ltd., the line agents in the UK. By this time the claim was time barred. The subsequent inquiry found no fault with the command of the **Olau Britannia** (I). However as there were common syndicates underwriting both ships hulls we were subjected to a marine knock for knock, with our insurers ending up paying 20%.

THE ZEEBRUGGE DISASTER

In the life of Olau one single event, the foundering of the **Herald of Free Enterprise** on the 6th March 1987 with the consequential appalling loss of life, had more direct influence on our trading activity than anything else to that point in time.

Suddenly, it seemed, everyone was an expert in ferry safety, the media was full of investigative journalism, much of it ill informed. The travelling public on the other hand assumed that all other ferries were operated in the same way as the ill fated Herald. The public voted with their feet in droves and the cost to Olau and all the other ferry operators was immeasurable in both financial terms and damage to our reputations. The media of course fanned the flames as that is what sells newspapers.

In response to the justified public outcry, legislation was rushed through by the Department of Transport (DoT) which specifically targeted the design and

operation of the type of ship operated by the then Townsend Thoresen which had just been acquired by P&O a few weeks before the tragedy. This involved controls on counting boarding passes, regulations regarding stability calculations and closed circuit television cameras on the car deck.

At Olau we already had boarding pass control, and had since 1976; the ships we operated at the time of the accident had built-in stability indicators for loading freight; and a ships' officer supervised the sealing of the ship which in any case the Captain could see, unlike the Herald Captain who was unsighted.

To comply with the new legislation we had to fit closed circuit television cameras on the car decks with the screens on the bridge to tell the Captain what he already knew; however there was an additional security spin off so the money was not completely wasted.

The next requirement was for a weighbridge to weigh all lorries before loading so the ship could be trimmed. Olau's ships had built in stability indicators in the form of two illuminated orange arrows positioned on the centre bulkhead. During loading if the ship was out of trim, one of the lights would go out indicating the situation to the loading officer but ballast tanks were also available for fine adjustment. The weigh tickets were printed out in the freight office and actually became used there to indicate a vehicle had arrived at the Port.

Olau Line had had boarding pass control since 1976

not only to check our licensed sailing figures but also for audit purposes in checking passenger tickets to the manifest. Our system involved issuing plastic boarding passes in different colours denoting the type of passage paid for which would be collected again by traffic controllers when boarding commenced. The collected passes would then be reconciled to the tickets, signed off and put back into stock. These passes were in a pre-numbered series which were switched at random as for a short while there was a black market in Olau boarding passes in some pubs in Sheerness. This system was not capable of retrospective audit however and so to comply with the new legislation we switched to card pre-numbered passes which were then sealed in a packet after each sailing.

Putting the tragedy into historical perspective, it is sadly part of our life today that people have to die to improve safety, which after all, should always be paramount in every case, before profit, before anything. Public safety is an obvious pre-condition for any ferry operator but there is no amount of legislation that could deal with the malaise that afflicted Townsend Thoresen at this time.

We should however remember that The Department of Transport (DoT) is ultimately responsible for all aspects of public transport in the UK and more particularly the safety of the travelling public. We also know that government departments never accept responsibility for their failings and whilst the Herald combination of circumstances were bizarre, nobody kept their eye on the ball. The ultimate responsibility rested with the Department of Transport.

Last year nine Americans travelling in a coach to Canterbury were killed near Faversham when their coach overturned; forgetting the vehicle defects for one moment everyone agrees that with seat belts at least the death toll would not have been so high. The coach industry know this but waits for an exact directive from the DoT on the type of belts. Inexplicably, the DoT dithers and more people will have to die before something is done. It is the same with air bags in cars, crash helmets for cyclists, and so on. The equation is death = public outcry = legislation. You cannot legislate against malaise but when a hazard is known and nothing is done it is the DoT who have the malaise.

More recently was the inquest into the M62 coach crash where the coroner urged the Government to legislate on mini bus seat belts. Incredibly Robert Key's response was that common sense would prevail and changes would automatically follow, a view I find crass in the extreme. For many years in this country all new cars had to be fitted with seat belts, first in the front and now in the back as well.

IT TOOK LEGISLATION HOWEVER TO MAKE PEOPLE USE THEM.

The DoT's job is to protect people from themselves.

At Olau, our ships were frequently inspected and certified by representatives of the country of registration and classification, Germany, plus the UK Department of Transport and also their Dutch equivalent. Hardly a month went by without some kind of spot inspection.

Every effort was made to make travelling by Olau as safe and comfortable as physically possible.

All other ferries plying from the UK are also subjected to the same vigorous scrutiny and hopefully the obscure disastrous combination of circumstances that caused the Herald disaster will never be allowed to recur. Britain, to her eternal credit, was at least the precursor in forcing new safety legislation on all ferry companies operating from the UK and ferry travel is significantly safer as a result.

Other European members of the International Maritime Organisation, The (IMO) were scornful of Britain's lead and in the main ignored the lessons learnt at Zeebrugge. The most recent mv **Estonia** disaster has eclipsed Zeebrugge in all aspects including the fact that it too was avoidable. Once again the media fields their usual array of misinformed experts who all forget that ferry travel is one of the safest most convienient means of transport.

The IMO must now wake up and unilaterally ensure that all members adopt the lessons learnt at Zeebrugge as a matter of utmost urgency.

AA FIVE STAR AWARDS

At Olau we always tried to be in the vanguard of change and always a change for the better but to get this across to the travelling public or the trade was a different matter. We were forever meeting people in Sittingbourne (ten miles from Sheerness) and the surrounding area who had never been to the Isle of Sheppey, let alone heard of Olau.

From this it is easy to conclude these people must either live in a hole or perhaps our sales department were completely incompetent. Perhaps the answer is simpler than that. I personally am not, for instance, interested in travelling anywhere by bus so as a consequence switch off to all bus and coach adverts; perhaps the same applies to ferries? On the other hand the travel trade whose business it is to know, frequently did not know either. I wonder what their excuse is?

Without a doubt the best thing that could have happened to us in recent years was the introduction by the Automobile Association of their AA star ferry awards in 1992. This was a brilliant marketing ploy and the brainchild of Graham Berville the then General Manager of the AA Retail Operations.

The awards were set up under a cloak of secrecy by the AA who had actually had their inspectors travel on all the ferries before they let on what they were doing; when the results were announced out of forty-five ferries assessed only five got the top rating of 5 stars and two were the **Olau Hollandia** (2) and **Olau Britannia** (2). The three other 5 star ships were the **Bretagne** of Brittany Ferries and the **Dana Anglia** and **Princess of Scandinavia** of DFDS.

The assessment ratings were based on onboard facilities and service which is where we at Olau had spent so much time and effort getting things right. We had at last received due recognition in a most credible way by a highly respected independent organisation, the AA.

Since 1992 the AA Ferry Guide has become the

Captain Peter Rodehache senior master of the **Olau Britannia** (2) accepting the 1992 AA five star award for his ship.

Captain Joachim Leu, Olau Line Commodore and master of **Olau Hollandia** (2) accepting the AA five star award for his ship.

industry bible, it is the Egon Ronay of the ferry business that now serves as a beacon for all operators who want to raise their standards to follow.

The effect of the AA five star awards on the other ferry businesses and the trade was electric. All those in the upper end of the market strove to raise their standards and star ratings which generally involved putting on new tonnage. The awards pointed the way forward and stimulated public demand for better standards; a measure of their success was that in 1993 6 ships got 5 stars, again including the two Olau ships and in 1994, the year of our demise, 9 ships received the 5 star accolade, the new winners all being new ships. The 9 five star ferries in 1994 were **Olau Hollandia** (2) and **Olau Britannia** (2), the **Bretagne, Normandie** and **Val de Loire** of Brittany Ferries (ex TT Line **Nils Holgersson**), **the Pride of Bilbao** of P&O, and finally the **Dana Anglia, Prince of Scandinavia and Princess of Scandinavia** of DFDS.

By chartering Olau's ships P&O acquired our five star ratings that went with them to become the **Pride of Le Havre** and the **Pride of Portsmouth** respectively.

By a cruel twist of fate the presentation of the 1994 awards by the AA to Case Rietkerk, on behalf of the Olau ships was on the 12th May 1994, the day the **Olau Britannia** (2) left Sheerness for the last time to go via Vlissingen to Le Havre and become the **Pride of Portsmouth.**

Olau can honestly claim that it has led the field in bringing Scandinavian style luxury to cross channel ferry operations but full recognition for this achievement only finally came through the AA and their 5 star awards which were the catalyst in triggering other operators to have the confidence to invest in new better tonnage.

The AA five star award is treasured by those that have it and envied by those that do not. It is a worthy accolade for promoting both the ferry and the route and re-assessed each year. At Olau we always claimed your holiday starts with the ferry, not from when you get off on the other side. Time seems to stand still at sea and on Olau ferries, unlike a plane or that hole in the ground, passengers were treated like people, could move about, eat real, rather than plastic, food and relax in luxurious surroundings. Too many people spend their time rushing about for their work, and a holiday is a time to slow down and enjoy yourself.

Although Olau is no more, our legacy is the greater comfort and ambience that is now more generally available and enjoyed by the travelling public on cross Channel ferries.

To modify another operator's slogan, they 'raised the standards', but we at Olau forced them to by creating a demand for something better.

BS5750 (or ISO9002)

One of the buzz words that has grown from recent EC legislation is the BS5750 accreditation also known as ISO9002 in European quarters.

Briefly this involves a Company writing a Janet & John instruction manual of their complete systems, and setting out every task and what quality checks are made to ensure the Company standard is maintained. This is almost to the point of saying pick up a pen, write with the sharp end of it, etc.

At Olau we looked at the requirement specification, and to be honest found ourselves wondering if they were serious, the thing went far beyond what was obvious. Initially, we frankly ridiculed the proposals and regarded the whole thing as another load of time wasting Brussels bunkum; indeed another good reason to be a Euro sceptic.

However as time passed more and more of our customers were attaining accreditation and what is more, asking if we had it. In the end it became like joining a Masonic lodge, everyone was hinting we should be in whilst denying it would affect our business, whilst we on our part thought the initiation ceremony frivolous.

In the end needs must and under pressure from our Vlissingen office and a number of our customers who moved chemicals we took the plunge and applied for accreditation which was granted on the 18th March 1994.

Looking back on the exercise we were obliged to create an office manual in far greater detail than would be normal. Staff hitherto at Olau were taught on a sit by Nellie basis, ie by someone who knows the job already and in small Olau (which was almost a family business) this had been the best grounding. There is nothing like being thrown in at the deep end to bring someone along.

The BS5750 accreditation in the end was perhaps not such a bad thing. It did force management and staff alike to analytically look at every procedure and make a decision as to how we wanted it done in the future.

The finished manual would have formed the basis of new employees' job descriptions but it was not to be. The certificate was collected by John Lawson our Freight Manager on 18th May 1994 three days after our last sailing and by which time most of our staff had

been made redundant.

Life is like that.

MONOPOLIES COMMISSION

In the summer of 1988 P&O European Ferries and Stena Sealink made an application to the Department of Trade to pool their resources on certain short sea routes to strengthen themselves against the expected onslaught from the Channel Tunnel.

The Department of Trade referred the matter to the Monopolies Commission who invited all other ferries to make representations.

Shortly afterwards Case Rietkerk and I accepted their invitation to meet the Commission at their offices round the back of The Law Courts in Central London. The building was disappointing, just another faceless Government Department with the now obligatory security officers and current security level notice. Whilst waiting in their austere foyer we pondered Sir David Frost's ultimate enigma, 'Why is there only 'one' Monopolies Commission?'

Exactly on time we were duly summoned to the Government equivalent of a penthouse suite. We were seated behind a huge bench/table that already carried large place tags with our names. Mine was spelt correctly whilst Case's was wrong which was unusual, normally it was the other way round.

At the other end of the room was a similar bench/table and there were four on the panel with one vacant chair, it reminded me of SPECTRE in the James Bond stories, particularly with the vacant chair. The chairman introduced himself and the panel and explained that we had as long as we wanted to make our representations which would be taken down by a stenographer.

They would question us as required and we would later receive a transcript which we could check, edit etc. He explained that if we wanted we could add to, amend or delete anything we had said if we wished on this transcript until we were happy that it fairly reflected our position. Above all, it seemed, they intended to be fair and seen to be fair.

We argued our case that the P&O/Stena offer was flawed as the Channel Tunnel, was, in 1988, some years off completion. As it happened much further than everyone thought at the time. (At Olau we expected it to be late, so much so that I was running a book on the start date for fare paying passengers.) Collaboration at this early stage was in our view a gambit to make hay, or rather sacks of money, whilst the sun shone but more insidiously a ploy to effectively take control of the market before a new major competitor entered the fray.

Although the routes from Dover were not in direct competition to Olau, the utilisation of equipment that would follow rationalisation would drive all passenger and freight rates downwards as the monopoly effect took hold. On the passenger side, the undertakings to freeze brochure fares were worthless as most volume business through Dover travelled on contract rates which were not part of the proposed undertaking by P&O and Stena Sealink.

At some point in the proceedings, a fifth male

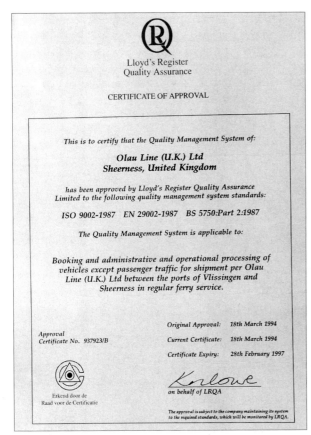

Our BS5750/ISO9002 Certificate dated, ironically, the 18th May 1994.

The 1994 AA five star awards for the **Olau Hollandia** (2) and **Olau Britannia** (2) that were earned but destined never to be hung on board.

A view of Dover Eastern Docks in Townsend days.

Olau Hollandia (2) lays on her Sheerness berth for the very last time on the 15th May 1994. This view shows clearly the Sheerness passenger walkway and the pod, which contained the gangway to the ship (Philippe Holthof).

member of the panel came in from a rear door rather unsteadily, took his seat and within a few minutes fell asleep. At the end of the hearing we had an opportunity to question the panel and we mischievously thought of putting a question to the now comatose No 2. However the Chairman was clearly embarrassed by his colleague so we left it at that. I wonder how much it pays to sleep on the Monopolies Commission and if they have any vacancies?

Despite the apparent scrupulous attempts to be fair we received the transcript of our presentation the day after we were supposed to have approved it. A protest bought us another day, and in fact no alterations were necessary but we kind of smelt a rat from then. After all we have all seen *Yes Minister* and learnt never to trust politicians, and in particular count your fingers when you get your hand back after shaking hands with one. Perhaps we were being hustled after all and the platitudes were all a smoke screen. Maybe the brief from the Minister was to go away and write me a report finding in favour of this proposal. Who knows?

The findings were published some months later. To the fury of P&O and Stena Sealink their application to work together was turned down for the time being at least. To our astonishment the tail had wagged the dog and little Olau, together with the other objectors, had got the application put on hold .

Surprisingly, to us at least, all subsequent attempts by the two protagonists to co-operate have also been denied which would seem to indicate a hidden political agenda here somewhere. Certainly we were not consulted again and our objections had only been fundamental as to the timing. Perhaps Sir Alistair Morton has a fairy God Mother somewhere after all who has arranged things so as to give the Channel Tunnel some luck, God knows it needs it. My money says it will require another large cash injection before it is fully operational. It will also, of course, be

someone else's fault.

Since the late 80's both petitioning ferry operators have considerably improved their services but in my personal view P&O are now head and shoulders ahead of Stena Sealink on the short sea routes. I further believe the raison d'être for a pooling arrangement is slipping away and that P&O would now be selling themselves short. Furthermore both operators have just set about cutting each other's throats again in a price war which, with no Channel Tunnel in the summer of 1994, is ill-conceived as they are just diminishing their own income. Perhaps they know something nobody else does but in the meantime all the balls are once again up in the air, and it is a case of watch this space.

The next few years however will see the final reckoning as the new SOLAS 90 (Safety of Life at Sea) rules are phased in. Many of the older ships currently plying the short sea routes will be beyond economical upgrading and fail to reach re-classification. At the same time the Channel Tunnel, when it eventually starts, will have carved itself out a share of the market; in my view taking most of it from Stena Sealink in the form of Classic Rail Passengers.

The new world order I believe will be that the ferries that remain will be of a very high standard indeed to contrast against the plastic austerity of the tunnel. Whilst there will also be a place for fast ferries these will be in the minority, expensive to build and operate, of low capacity and not able to operate in all weathers due to their fragile nature. Strength means weight and weight reduces speed so you are left with a normal ferry.

Interestingly though, although duty free is extended within the EC until 1999, Sir Alistair Morton has been given leave for a judicial review on the legality of this arrangement whilst conveniently forgetting that he too can sell duty free in his tunnel if he wishes. Certainly when duty free is abolished there will be no hidden subsidy for cross Channel ferry fares and the short sea routes and domestic airlines will see a massive hike in fares.

Olau's fare structure was not supported by Duty Free sales so we would not have felt this very much, had we still been around that is.

When the dust settles I believe that apart from the fast ferries one operator will remain and that will be P&O. The Monopolies Commission referral will then be an irrelevance and market forces will have done the work for them after all there is a saying that 99% of problems go away if you ignore them.

Chapter 8
THE FINAL CHAPTER

SEEBETRIEBSRAT
(sea workers' participation council)

The demise of Olau Line was almost entirely due to an odious piece of European legislation that forms part of the Maastricht Treaty, this is the so called Social Chapter sometimes referred to as Social Charter.

Everyone in the UK knows that first Margaret Thatcher and then John Major have stood alone in Europe in resisting this Socialist right of workers to participate in the running of a business. There is no problem with the concept but the practice, in the case of Olau, was to instil a cancer, that remorselessly ate away at our profitability. Our cancer was terminal so it was incurable, and the end was inevitable, simply a question of time.

The Social Chapter of the Maastricht Treaty deals with a number of questions of workers' rights and amongst other things guarantees a minimum wage and working week together with a right to have a Betriebsrat (on board ship a Seebetriebsrat), or workers' participation council.

Briefly in Germany, and Olau was a German Company, the law prescribes for elected worker participation. Any Company employing more than five people must, if the employees insist, set up a Betriebsrat or workers' participation council. These people are elected by the employees in a secret ballot and must be consulted on any matters that relate to employees terms and conditions which you would expect but more importantly on investment plans, reorganisation, training, recruitment, holidays in fact nearly every aspect of the business that would normally be a Director's decisions.

In theory the Betriebsrat cannot block anything, they merely have to be consulted, but the reality is very different. At Olau, in the end, we could not change the brand of toilet paper without notice and consent from the Betriebsrat.

As a German Company our head office in Hamburg had to provide an office for three full time elected representatives of the Seebetriebsrat plus secretarial assistance, free use of all facilities and re-imbursement of travelling expenses. We were effectively forced to have these people on our premises on our payroll to screw up the business, nothing more nothing less.

The Seebetriebsrat on their part embarked on a crusade of probing every aspect of the Company's organisation with a view to their members on the ships working less time for more pay with consequential increase in manning levels. To this end they worked tirelessly, neutralising all other costs savings throughout the group, and under the misplaced view that our shareholders were some sort of philanthropic society.

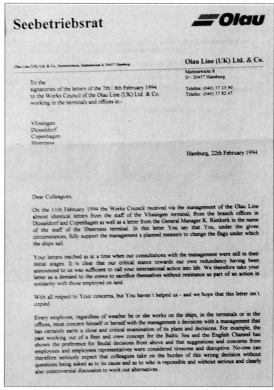

A Seebetriebsrat letter to Olau staff members. Note the formal address of our head office, including telephone and fax. This is how it had to be, by law, by the Social Chapter.

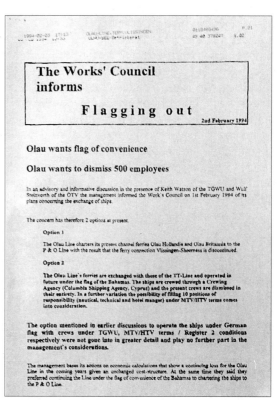

A militant letter from the Workers' Council on flagging out.

The real trouble had started when the Olau shareholders took up their option to build **Olau Hollandia** (2) and **Olau Britannia** (2) but opted to enter them under the second German Register. The first two Olau ships were under the normal German Register as that was all there was in 1981 and 1982.

The Bundes Republik of Deustchland had introduced the so called second Register as, like other European countries, it was becoming increasingly concerned at seeing more and more of its merchant fleet flagging out to flags of convenience. The second Register was a half way house created under political pressure to stem this exodus, and permitted a certain number of non German Nationals on board ship in non essential duties such as cleaning and catering. This was heresy to the German OTV.

The OTV (German Transport Union) were furious at this new legislation and through their members exercised their right to set up a Seebetriebsrat on both the new Olau ships. The first demand, before the ships were even built, was that all crew members should have individual cabins irrespective of whether on board or not. In this context all crew were 'paired' from the Captain's to AB's (able bodied seamen); officers had individual cabins on the old ships but normally other crew would share a two berth cabin although neither occupant would be in residence together. The Company wanted to provide larger two berth cabins for all crew but were forced to settle for individual much smaller units at of course greater cost. This was just the start! Like a child who gets a sweet every time he asks, so the Seebetriebsrat scaled up their demands and although an element of negotiation took place the result always cost Olau more money in the perhaps naive hope that it would end there. It never did of course, it never does.

The Olau ships had about one third English crew, about one third German and one third multinational. Generally the German crew were on the engineering and navigation side with most of the rest on catering with a few German officers. The British crew were not involved at all in this save that by accepting a Seebetriebsrat recommendation/edict that all transfers of job, no matter how temporary, were channelled through the Seebetriebsrat, they effectively gave up control of their destiny.

In practice this meant that Olau could not transfer a waitress, for example, for a half day from say the restaurant to the cafeteria. By channelling all requests through the Seebetriebsrat the consequential delay (days) negated any benefit. The hours of work on board ship set down by the Seebetriebsrat generated over manning and despite the fact there were 120-150 crew on board passengers would normally only see about 10-15 at work at any one time. There were of course as many at work behind the scenes in catering and the engine room but significantly less than half of the total which is what you would normally expect.

IN THE END OUR SUPERB FIVE STAR SHIPS WERE EFFECTIVELY BEING RUN FOR THE CONVENIENCE OF SOME MEMBERS OF THE CREW, NOT FOR THE BENEFIT OF OUR PASSENGERS OR THE SHIPS' SHAREHOLDERS.

PROJECT OLAU

By March 1993 it was becoming increasingly apparent that the Port of Sheerness was more interested in their share price than their customers and we at Olau had to seriously look around at how we could make our new big ships pay their way.

With a lousy road access from the M2 and a Port that had priced us out of the market, we started avidly searching for alternative opportunities. The Olau Board in Hamburg in the meantime tried their own coup to re-flag the ships to Luxembourg over a weekend. If successful this would have made the big ships profitable but it was not to be. Unfortunately due to a technical omission in the paperwork, the Seebetriebsraat were able to get a German Judge to order a return to the German second register. We apparently only had one chance at this re-flagging option which was now dead in the water.

It therefore came about that by the summer of 1993 we were in serious talks with London Thames Terminals for moving our service to Dartford. Rumours of course were rife but all at Olau remained tight lipped, PROJECT OLAU was born.

The key to this was that given our current overheads, and the obstructive Seebetriebsrat included, we needed another 100,000 passengers and 10-20 thousand freight units to make the route viable. We all agreed that this would not be possible without a decent road access and a Port who took a long term view on their customers. In fact the upgrading of the A249 to a dual carriageway was on the cards, but at that time the final announcement had not been made, and even if it had been, its completion in two years would be two years too late for Olau.

The Port of Sheerness in the meantime continued to extract maximum payment from us for a minimum commitment of manpower with virtually no maintenance taking place unless something physically stopped working. Our coach park was full of crevices and the answer from the Port was always that they would try to repair it in next year's budget.

We had also looked at the Ports of Dover and Tilbury but for various reasons felt they were not quite right for us.

The Port of Dartford by contrast to Sheerness, at least, had a positive attitude, it had excellent road links and was on the outskirts of London. We could have become London's only ferry to the continent, OLAU LONDON FERRIES, with potential, to use river taxis to connect to our hotels in central London.

A risk assessment concluded we would lose virtually no traffic but enter a new market with enormous potential; 16 million people lived within 1 hour and twenty minutes of Dartford, the world was on our doorstep. Virtually all the freight that went to Sheerness, Ramsgate, Dover, Folkestone and the Channel Tunnel had to pass Dartford, the opportunity would be manna from heaven.

Dartford Council welcomed us with open arms and nothing was too much trouble. I mention this as for many years Swale Borough Council had a down on Sheppey which was also mirrored in Kent County Council. In fairness to both bodies they have been most supportive in the last ten years but some genuine help in the early years when we most needed it may have changed the whole course of history. It is always the same, you do not know what you have until you lose it, and then it is invariably too late.

In December 1993 a full presentation was made to our board who welcomed the initiative and authorised us to proceed to contract stage. Planning permission in the meantime was granted for our new ferry terminal at Dartford in January 1994 and things really started to move but in a somewhat unexpected way.

At the same time our sister company TT Line had seen its passenger trade decimated in the Baltic by a new competitor, Euroway, who had entered their market some two years earlier by rate dumping. TT line had held their nerve knowing Euroway would go broke which they duly did at the end of 1993. Suddenly TT Line were faced with their market being restored but without the equipment to take advantage of it; their two ferries only had a capacity of 1100 passengers against Olau's 1600.

Each ship in the group had its own Partenreederei shareholders but the major share holdings were common to all four ships albeit in slightly different proportions. In January 1994 the shareholders took the decision to switch the ships, so they could take advantage of the new market in the Baltic, and give Olau the two smaller ships of 1100 passenger capacity.

This gave us at Olau a big problem, as we felt the kudos of going to Dartford with the largest and best ships on the Channel would be lost. The two ships on offer were converted freighters, with a reduced passenger capacity, although the passenger accommodation was to a very high standard indeed.

They were also slower which put the timetable in jeopardy, and the ports under pressure to turn the ships round quickly. One of these ships flew the German flag whilst the other was registered in the Bahamas with a multinational crew.

The proposed switch galvanised the Seebetriebsrat into action; they were resolutely against our management and were totally dedicated to increasing the number of crew, shortening their working hours and introducing as many restrictive practices as possible on board ship. In short they were behaving as unions did in the UK in the 1970's but with the backing of the German Law and the wretched Social Chapter.

All our efforts ashore to reduce costs were immediately absorbed by additional costs of working onboard. They believed in Workers' Power and that is what it was. Incredibly the workers' council were also more than prepared to compromise passenger safety, a situation which was totally unacceptable under any circumstances. A showdown was not only inevitable but now assumed a different urgency.

Although TT-Line wanted our ships they did not want the cancer that came with them and negotiations proceeded with the Seebetriebsrat for flagging both ships out to the Bahamas flag. In March 1994 the **Olau Britannia** (2) went into dry dock for its annual refit/overhaul and we ran with the **Olau Hollandia** (2) and a chartered freight ship.

Not wholly unexpectedly **Olau Hollandia** (2) went on strike in Vlissingen on the weekend of the 12th March 1994 just before the **Olau Britannia** (2) was due out of dry dock. Captain Leu, the Master and Line Commodore was imprisoned on board and the ship closed up.

The up river berth at Dartford International Ferry Terminal with the Queen Elizabeth Bridge in the background.

The front page of Lloyd's List 16th March 1994

Tough negotiations continued for over a week, until the shareholders called enough and put the ships up for sale or charter; this being the only way under German Law to now get rid of the cursed Seebetriebsrat once and for all.

P&O European Ferries had been sniffing round our ships for over two years by now, as they wanted to take on Brittany Ferries on the Western Channel and a very generous deal was eventually struck for them to charter both the Olau ships with the loss of 690 jobs at Olau. This was effectively a Kamikaze suicide pact by the Seebetriebsrat to take everyone else down with them.

Our shareholders, for once, found themselves in a win-win situation; if negotiations succeeded on flagging out they made the savings they needed and got rid of the obstructive Seebetriebsrat once and for all, or if they accepted the lucrative charter offer from P&O they got rid of them as well along with everyone else but with a very short pay back.

Although we all lost our jobs, our shareholders decision to have a showdown was long overdue and if I am honest with myself I would have done exactly the same in their invidious position. There was a time to say enough, and this was the time.

Case Rietkerk described this 'as an act of industrial vandalism, the unions had done what our competitors had failed to do for so many years, put us out of business'. The strike was over on the 20th March and both ships returned to normal service until the 12th May 1994 when the **Olau Britannia** (2) left us followed by the **Olau Hollandia** (2) on the 15th May, 1994 when the route closed.

There was one final sting in the tail, when the settlement agreement became known. Our shareholders were prohibited from participating in Olau Line again and had to indemnify the union against any claims arising out of the strike, such as false imprisonment of the Captain and libel damages where outrageous false statements were made to the press. The fact that the Union extracted this indemnity is in itself an admission of guilt condoning their extreme tactics.

As there were no suitable ships available, which was why P&O wanted ours, we were dead. Not only were we faced with finding ships we also required new backers as our shareholders had been forced to agree to pull out in order to end the occupation of the **Olau Hollandia** (2). Project Olau, the move to Dartford, was thus killed off, even though by this time we were virtually at contract stage with London Thames Terminals. That the Port of Sheerness would have lost Olau was certain as is the Government report criticising the £70 million profit made by a few people following the privatisation of the Medway Ports Authority. Perhaps in the end this was Ted Heath's unacceptable face of capitalism at work.

Putting these events in historical perspective, it is easy to see why our shareholders had had enough. They are not and were not in the ferry business to provide employment for trade union activists. They were hard headed institutional investors who were investing funds, including pension fund money, in businesses which give a return on capital employed. The outrageous almost hysterical demands from the Seebetriebsraat to order new ships, increase manning and so on had no basis in the real world. Running ships of our standard where the Seebetriebsrat decide the opening hours of the restaurants, and who works where was beyond belief, a problem that has not transferred to P&O who are now 'open all hours' and can properly capitalise on their five year charter.

It is perhaps sad that the German OTV Union whose members made up our Seebetriebsrat did not have some of their pension fund money in our ships. If they had the boot may have been on the other foot.

Germany as a country is where we were in the 1970's in the UK. The worm will turn one day but for the time being the OTV have made sure it will be a long, long, time before anyone puts a ship under a German Flag again, first or second Register.

OLAU LINE
Rest In Peace

Once we got the ships back it was business as usual until mid-May. However we had an enormous number of forward bookings which had to be cancelled or re-routed which became quite a logistical exercise.

Swale Borough Council were stunned and it seemed

TT Line m.v. **Peter Pan** which together with her sister the m.v. **Nils Holgersson** were to be swapped for the **Olau Hollandia** (2) and **Olau Britannia** (2) (Olau Collection)

The Directors and Staff of Olau Line wish to thank all customers and suppliers for their loyal support over the past 19 years.

We are proud that with your help we have created the best ferry service across the Channel.

Regrettably, due to circumstances beyond our control, this service ceased on May 15th, 1994.

Olau

SHEERNESS (KENT) ⇌ VLISSINGEN (HOLLAND) • OLAU LINE (UK) LTD., SHEERNESS, KENT ME12 1SN

All good things come to an end!

We had fun while it lasted - we hope you did too.

Olau

The above notice was placed in Travel Trade Gazette the week after the closure of Olau Line.

The **Olau Hollandia** (2) on her berth at Sheerness for the last time on the morning of the 15th May 1994

Olau's administration office in Sheerness was the Old Paymasters House from Royal Dockyard days which came complete with the ghost of the Old Paymaster who was apparently murdered there. This building was a fire damaged leaking shell until refurbished by Olau to its former glory.

The Olau press release dated 23rd March 1994 announced the closure of the Sheerness-Vlissingen ferry service after nearly 20 years.

to take an age for them to come to terms with the consequences. We could all use our fingers and work out the direct job losses to the Borough but they seemed to have a paralysis of grasping the implications of the cash that would disappear from circulation in the Borough and the consequences of that on the local economy. Furthermore, Tesco were building a new hyper market just outside the Sheerness docks entrance scheduled for opening ironically the week after we closed.

The Port of Sheerness dithered as well, Olau had established a viable freight route to Vlissingen and whilst no suitable passenger ships were currently available, (we know we looked), they could have, and should have, put on a freight ship within days to maintain the route. Although they have now done this they also have to fight to get back traffic lost to other ports.

Olau Line is now part of history and before my dotage arrives I felt compelled to write this book. I have tried to show how different Olau was to any other Company I have known. It belonged, it was special and that is a tribute to all past and present staff both direct and indirect who helped give flesh and body to Olau a living Company.

I hope you have enjoyed reading this book as much as I have writing it, and I further hope you will now remember Olau Line, what we stood for, and what we achieved. I will.

Positively the last Olau Line passenger boarding **Olau Hollandia (2)** on the 15th May 1994. The ship was full and sailed uncharacteristically half an hour late due to the many go-shows that turned up at the last minute.

Escorted by Knight's navy (sorry Alexander tugs navy) the **Olau Hollandia** (2) with her decks packed like a troop ship, moves to turn in the Medway.

Always a showman at heart, Captain Mantei turns and stops to salute Sheerness in the time honoured fashion.

The **Olau Hollandia** (2) sails into history to become the **Pride of Le Havre**. Case Rietkerk, in a small motor launch, led the **Olau Hollandia (**2) down the Medway Channel to the Medway buoy before signalling a final farewell.

The cover of Holiday Which for March 1984. They said of Olau 'The **Hollandia** and **Britannia** are the best boats we saw all summer. The standard of decor in the seating and restaurants is excellent, and the range of entertainments includes dancing, indoor swimming pool, sauna and gaming tables. There is a good range of comfortable spacious cabins.' Actually 'boats are carried on 'ships' but apart from this minor slip this is flattery indeed. Remember this was in 1984 with **Olau Hollandia** (I) and **Olau Britannia** (I).

In March 1992 they said of Olau, - 'Flag ships - the best afloat. The two ships on the Sheerness-Vlissingen route are in a class of their own - winners of four of our five special awards'.

Dear Mr Rietkerk

Thank you very much for the farewell trip on the OLAU HOLLANDIA and OLAU BRITANNIA. We had a lovely day. we will miss the ships very much. Heel hartelijk bedankt. My mummy is dutch and comes from Vlissingen.

Love from Alexander Hobbs

OLE LAURITZEN

23, ONSGAARDSVEJ
DK-2900 HELLERUP
TEL. 01-62 19 62

Case Rietkerk &
the Olau-Line Crew

10th May 1994

This week will be a sad one, for you and for me.

Suddenly the line you have worked for so long will
stop, and   a great enterprise will no longer exist.

I shall look back to the years we did work together
with fondness, because I found it a great pleasure
to have you as employees and partners. It was really
great fun!

I felt that I knew you all, and was happy when I met you
in Sheerness or on the ferries, where I could recollect
the good times we did have together – but also the
stress, hard work and debates (sometimes)

I realize that the closure of Olau-Line will be a hard
turningpoint for those, who have spent a lifetime with
the company and who will not have many job opportunities
in the future. I wish I could help.

I did consider to enlist interested parties, but when I
heard of the final decision, it was too late. I simply could
not believe it. A route with an excellent reputation (except
for the wildcatstrikes this year) and with many passengers
booked for the summer and much freight should not have
been shut down just like that.

But it has happened, and we can do nothing about it.

We can only look back to a job you have all done exceedingly
well, and to the many happy days we have had together.

I certainly look back at the first years with happiness and
I am proud that you have been so kind to me even after our
partnership ceased.

I wish you all the best for the future, I would have liked to
be on the very last Olau-Line ferry trip, but it would have
been too sad to see all your friendly faces and realize that
this would be the last time we sent off a ferry to Holland.

Yours affectionately

STATISTICS 1975-1994

	1975	1976	1977	1978	1979	1980	1981	1982	1983	1984
Trailers	6381	6364	10477	12785	20600	20285	24667	30011	26179	22608
Accompanied freight	6748	10377	13193	13056	15096	13259	17791	18477	23650	23646
Trade Cars	4486	6244	5465	6690	4141	1725	2606	43778	74672	69056
Miscellaneous	0	92	274	283	286	0	79	220	24	36
Passenger cars	36812	65093	60151	60365	58612	64020	74171	89261	108277	105319
Coaches	530	1582	1974	2514	2572	2576	3139	4755	5377	5102
Caravans	1497	504	784	884	669	540	1104	1320	739	549
Campers/trailers	235	1300	1118	991	811	1004	1163	2003	1507	1220
Bikes	1801	7512	6841	6613	6420	5667	5212	5108	5102	5229
Motorcycles	1100	2218	2214	2636	2640	1859	1599	1945	1804	1733
Passengers	220416	439708	424244	488773	457572	452109	533353	615813	581341	635891
Drivers	3820	11598	15950	14667	16659	15712	21638	22870	29052	29554

	1985	1986	1987	1988	1989	1990	1991	1992	1993	1994	GRAND TOTALS
Trailers	27120	29362	31819	38698	39042	35825	29640	24458	21606	6254	464181
Accompanied freight	27191	28676	28496	33937	35930	40681	41998	41619	40131	11934	485886
Trade Cars	71384	42459	34249	51588	51933	58041	43252	20361	5189	3533	600852
Miscellaneous	90	191	81	117	35	0	0	0	0	0	1808
Passenger cars	106399	115337	103547	124090	114717	123395	134246	130257	108512	25192	1807773
Coaches	5088	4686	3937	4200	4022	4660	4920	5212	4300	1041	72187
Caravans	450	447	351	445	399	1589	1362	1572	1124	159	16488
Campers/trailers	1414	998	982	1251	1164	1465	1712	1519	1585	272	23714
Bikes	3017	2825	2615	3154	2745	4302	4724	3994	4154	315	87350
Motorcycles	940	1143	834	1646	2240	2353	2766	3196	3100	285	38251
Passengers	643780	626136	534108	637861	627435	755509	800509	756636	673522	181514	11086230
Drivers	35394	37365	36889	41727	43155	48076	50637	49394	46878	13589	584624

SHIPS IN SERVICE

Ships in Service	Tonnage	Registered	Started Olau	Left Olau	Length	Width	Pax Capacity
Basto V	1877	Norway	20/11/74	15/3/75	87m	18m	250
Olau West	3242	Denmark	19/1/75	11/77	98m	18m	600
Olau East	3242	Denmark	16/3/75	24/11/75	98m	18m	600
Olau Dana	7672	Denmark	8/11/75	5/76	125m	19m	1100
Olau Kent	4238	Denmark	1/4/76	9/9/80	109m	17m	860
Olau Finn	7978	Finland	1/5/76	7/5/92	141m	21m	1400
Espresso Olbia	7338	Italy	2/10/80	24/3/81	138m	22m	1000
Olau Hollandia (1)	14990	Germany	25/3/81	3/10/89	152m	24.2m	1600
Olau Britannia (1)	14990	Germany	8/5/82	20/5/90	152m	24.2m	1600
Olau Hollandia (2)	35000	Germany	4/10/89	15/5/94	161m	29m	1600
Olau Britannia (2)	35000	Germany	21/10/90	12/5/94	161m	29m	1600

ACKNOWLEDGEMENTS

The other managers of Olau Line Sheerness, for their support and clarification of my memory, John Lawson, Pat Williams, Keith Russell, Nigel Ellinor and Ron Keefe.

Case Rietkerk for support and giving me first option on any historical records.

Barry Goddard, Duty Free Federation.

John Hendy for correcting my English.

Miles Cowsill for constructive advice on my book plan.

John Wilmshurst and Robin Hawkins for a first book review.

Trevor Stevens of Stevens Secunda for supplying original Olau artwork and advice.

Jean Kittle, Carol Tumber and Susan Holmes for hours of proof reading.

Ole Lauritzen for creating Olau and kindly allowing me to reproduce his letter.

My wife, Brenda letting me off the washing up to write this book.

David Sevier, my solicitor for deleting the many libellous parts.

Captain Mantei and Captain Heilmann.

Ken Page retired Director of the Passenger Shipping Association for encouragement.

Ian Carruthers of Brittany Ferries for clarification of pilotage.

Ian Collier of Lloyd's Bank for not calling in my overdraft.